Library of Congress Cataloging in Publication Data

Main entry under title:

Mexico and the United States.

(A Spectrum Book)
At head of title: The American Assembly,
Columbia University.
Background papers prepared for the Binational
American Assembly on Mexican-American Relations
held at Arden House, Harriman, N.Y., from Oct.
30-Nov. 2, 1980.
Includes-index.
Contents: Preface / William H. Sullivan—The
United States and Mexico / Robert McBride—Energy
issues in Mexico / Juan Eibenschutz—[etc.]
1. United States—Relations (general) with
Mexico—Congresses.   2. Mexico—Relations (general)
with the United States—Congresses.   I. American
Assembly.   II. Binational American Assembly on
Mexican-American Relations (1980: Harriman, N.Y.)
E183.8.M6M46   972.08'3   81-5171
ISBN   0-13-579565-6   AACR2
ISBN   0-13-579557-5 (pbk.)

The excerpt on page 158 from *Managing in Turbulent Times* by Peter F. Drucker is reprinted by permission of Harper & Row, Publishers, Inc. Copyright © 1980 by Peter F. Drucker.

Editorial/production supervision by Betty Neville
Manufacturing buyer: Barbara A. Frick

10   9   8   7   6   5   4   3   2   1

This Spectrum Book can be made available to businesses and organizations at a special discount when ordered in large quantities. For more information, contact:

Prentice-Hall, Inc.
General Book Marketing
Special Sales Division
Englewood Cliffs, New Jersey 07632

PRENTICE-HALL INTERNATIONAL, INC. (*London*)
PRENTICE-HALL OF AUSTRALIA PTY. LIMITED (*Sydney*)
PRENTICE-HALL OF CANADA, LTD. (*Toronto*)
PRENTICE-HALL OF INDIA PRIVATE LIMITED (*New Delhi*)
PRENTICE-HALL OF JAPAN, INC. (*Tokyo*)
PRENTICE-HALL OF SOUTHEAST ASIA PTE. LTD. (*Singapore*)
WHITEHALL BOOKS LIMITED (*Wellington, New Zealand*)

087099

 The American Assembly, *Columbia Un*

MEXICO
AND
THE UNITED STATES

Prentice-Hall, Inc., *Englewood Cliffs, New Jersey*

Table of Contents

Preface

During most of the period following World War II, the focus of United States foreign policy has been upon the superpower rivalry with the Soviet Union and the ancillary relationships of the cold war. Our public has tended to view other nations in the light of their affiliations in the global ideological struggle. Strategic considerations have been dominant in our perceptions of the world around us.

One consequence of this posture has been the neglect of our close, neighborly relations with Mexico, which have not previously figured greatly into the strategic balance, but which deserve careful management because of their intimate nature. Recent developments, particularly our concern with our heavy dependence on imported oil, have caused many Americans to become more acutely aware of the importance of Mexico to the future well-being of the United States.

Unfortunately, this new awakening of interest in Mexico has, to many United States citizens, been directed primarily toward Mexico's petroleum resources. Moreover, it often has been couched in suggestions that some sort of "deal" could be struck between Mexico and the United States which would assure us of continued access to Mexico's vast petroleum reserves.

Because The American Assembly feels that relations between Mexico and the United States have a broad, persistent, and pervasive character which must be constantly tended and carefully nourished, we convened the *Binational American Assembly on Mexican-American Relations* at Arden House in Harriman, New York, from October 30 through November 2, 1980. Sixty-five residents of Mexico and the United States met to discuss a series of papers prepared under the editorial supervision of the Honorable Robert H. McBride, former United States ambassador to Mexico, who acted as director for this Assembly. These papers have been compiled into this present volume, which is published as a stimulus to further discussion of this subject among informed and concerned citizens.

The opinions expressed in this volume are those of the individual authors and not necessarily those of The American Assembly, which does not take a stand on the topics it presents for public discussion. The same caveat applies to those foundations and corporations whose generous donations made this Assembly possible. They are the Celanese Corporation, William H. Donner Foundation, Dow Chemical Latin America, Exxon Corporation, General Motors Corporation, Andrew W. Mellon Foundation, Atlantic Richfield Foundation, Rockefeller Foundation, Tinker Foundation, TRW Foundation, and Xerox Fund Corporation.

William H. Sullivan
President
The American Assembly

Robert H. McBride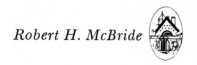

1

The United States and Mexico

The Shape of the Relationship

To set the tone and develop a cohesive pattern of U.S.–Mexican relations is difficult. Everywhere there is dichotomy and paradox. Contrasts occur constantly and new events superimpose themselves frequently.

A Historical Note

Before passing to a more general examination of U.S.–Mexican relations at the official level, it might be worth reviewing, however briefly, the well-known cultural and historical differences between the two nations. It is assumed that readers are aware of the historical conflicts from the war in 1846 virtually until World War II, the trauma

ROBERT H. MCBRIDE *spent thirty-four years in the U.S. Foreign Service, including posts in the Caribbean, western Europe, and North Africa. He served as ambassador in Zaire from 1967 to 1969 and Mexico from 1969 to 1974. While in Mexico, Ambassador McBride successfully negotiated the Border Treaty of 1970 and the Salinity Treaty of 1973. Since leaving government service he has served as diplomat-in-residence on the faculty of the University of Virginia, director of the Princeton University Alumni Forum, and lecturer on Latin America at Dartmouth College. He has published numerous articles on Mexican-American relations and is founder of the Inter-American Council on Manpower and Development.*

this has caused Mexico, and their continuing background role in Mexican thinking. Added to that are the profoundest differences in cultural origins, brought out in brilliant detail in an article published in 1979 in *The New Yorker* by Octavio Paz. He goes far beyond the usual platitudes regarding our differing outlook and traces the distinct origins of our two peoples, the U.S. originally and for many years being dominated by English culture, and Mexico by Spanish or Latin approaches to cultural values, human activity, etc. Upon this original variation, detailed by Paz, are superimposed later—and now false— images of Mexico in the U.S. as the land of the sombrero-wearing dozer under a cactus. The issue is not really whether or not the U.S. viewpoint changes, but rather when it catches up with the reality of modern Mexico.

Therefore, any study must be based on recognition of Mexican atti- tudes resulting from history, as well as deep fundamental differences in our peoples. Obviously the advent of large numbers of Mexicans to this country, in which they will play an increasingly important role, will change attitudes somewhat. History and cultural background, however, certainly cannot be ignored yet as influences molding U.S.- Mexican relations. In fact, recent differences between Washington and Mexico City, superimposed on old ones, have led a leading observer and expert, Dr. Olga Pellicer, to question whether old-fashioned ap- proaches to negotiating out the major issues can really succeed at this juncture. I have added somewhat to her reasoning to wonder if the 1980s may not possibly be the decade of "damage control"—preventing the atmosphere from getting worse in the hope that more definitive solutions can be achieved at a later time and under different condi- tions.

Some patterns have emerged clearly during the period dating from when two Presidents took office almost simultaneously (Jimmy Carter in January 1977 and Jose Lopez Portillo in December 1976). Even earlier, during the second half of the Echeverría administration (1974–76), the overall trend of U.S.–Mexican relationships, which had been improving more or less steadily since 1940, had began to deteri- orate. The improvement over the disastrous heritage of the nineteenth century, when Mexico lost over half of her territory to the U.S., prob- ably began under the impetus of World War II. Serious difficulties had continued well into the twentieth century, despite one upturn during the Lincoln-Júarez period. Whatever the background, one can theorize that the period from 1940 to 1974 was overall the most positive period in the dealings of the two neighboring nations.

By arbitrarily selecting a date of 1974 for the "end of an era," could one be led to conclude that the more recent years have seen a decline? Perhaps more important, if new tensions have arisen, what are the prospects for their alleviation in the new decade? It is these two questions which this chapter will attempt to examine.

The Echeverría Administration: 1970 to 1976

Perhaps the first development to study is the position and attitude of President Echeverría. During the first half, roughly 1970–73, of his administration the previous encouraging impetus largely continued. However, from the onset President Echeverría had publicly announced a need for independence from the United States. In policy terms, in the economic field, this led to increased demands for diversification of Mexican markets and trading patterns. In the political field, there was a call for more "independent" policies and courses of action in accord with Third World aspirations.

During earlier Mexican administrations, it had often occurred to the Department of State that Mexico could play a useful role in hemispheric "bridge-building," for instance, by taking a more active part in Central American activities. This of course envisaged a case where Mexico and U.S. foreign policies were congruent. So a greater Mexican role in Latin America was not a new idea.

Under Echeverría, it became Mexican policy to some extent to be more active, and he exchanged visits with all of the heads of state of the Central American countries fairly quickly. On one occasion, early in the *sexenio* ("six-year term"), then Foreign Secretary Emilio Rabasa indicated to the U.S. that perhaps Mexico could play a useful part in U.S. negotiations with Panama, at that juncture stalled. This particular initiative did not suit Washington, however, which believed only direct, bilateral discussions could be productive.

Echeverría made his initial state visit, early in 1971, to President Allende in Chile. This visit was returned with considerable fanfare in 1972. The Mexican President had studied earlier in Chile and felt a considerable kinship there. However, the Mexican relationship with Allende was not appreciated much in Washington, although the Mexican tie with Castro—never broken despite the resolution of the Organization of American States calling on its members to sever relations with Cuba—had long been accepted. The Mexican tie with Cuba indeed did prove useful to the U.S. in the Habana-Matamoros refugee airlift of the 1960s. This was vastly smaller than the more publicized Varadero-Miami shuttle, but nevertheless was the source of escape from Cuba for thousands of individuals, including U.S. citizens. The passengers who landed at Matamoros in Aeromexico planes, cost reimbursed by the Department of State, subsequently crossed the border to Brownsville, Texas. The airlift was amicably discontinued when there seemed to be few additional sources of passengers in 1972.

However, not only did President Echeverría establish a friendly relationship with Allende, but Santiago was the locale for his first announcement of the Charter of Economic Rights and Duties of Nations. This eventually led to a serious incident between Mexico City and Washington, D.C., which perhaps started the deterioration of relations. When this document was studied in Washington, it became apparent that its basic philosophy was unacceptable in terms of U.S. government policies and precedents. Calling for billions of dollars to be turned over by the developed countries to the developing countries, via the United Nations, it virtually eliminated national controls over expenditures. Since U.S. aid programs, from the Marshall Plan to the present, have invariably called for congressional and other supervision of disbursements, via end use checks and other mechanisms, it was quickly concluded in Washington that, regrettably, the Echeverría program was a nonstarter for the U.S. Despite suggestions from the U.S. that the Congress would not approve disbursement of funds under such a framework, Echeverría pressed forward, and the charter was presented to the United Nations where it was passed by a huge majority in the General Assembly. The negative votes were limited to those of the giant Western industrial powers: the United States, the Federal Republic of Germany, Japan, etc.

A vigorous debate took place in the executive branch of the U.S. government on this initiative. Henry Kissinger, by this time secretary of state, and with an extraordinarily close rapport with Mexican Foreign Secretary Rabasa, had urged acceptance, whereas William Simon, secretary of the treasury, had more realistically recommended a "no" vote. Frequently the compromise is an abstention. But in this case the more accurately reflective negative vote at the U.N. led to considerable bitterness in the Mexican government by 1974.

The second half of the Echeverría administration became an unhappy time in Mexican-American relations. In the first years of the 1970s, a number of specific negotiable issues—even though negotiable with difficulty—had been settled. Specifically, the Border Agreement of 1970, announced by Presidents Nixon and Díaz Ordaz at Puerto Vallarta, and the Salinity Treaty of 1973 had terminated issues that were of long-standing nuisance value, and which had themselves seemed for a time insoluble. These were settled, especially in the case of the Colorado River salinity, with the aid of the U.S. Congress and at expense to the U.S. taxpayer. The Border Treaty ended all remaining land and maritime border disputes. It also provided a mechanism for settling any further disputes that could arise from changes in the course of the Rio Grande. The Salinity Treaty ended a long controversy over the quality of water delivered to Mexico by the U.S. from the Colorado River. The waters were so salty that agriculture was impossible on the Mexican side, apparently violating a U.S.–Mexican treaty of 1940.

Both treaties received near unanimous votes in the U.S. Senate. By 1974, we were down to old problems—trade imbalance, for example—which were endemic and perhaps only manageable, not soluble. The problem of undocumented Mexican workers in the U.S. began to grow rapidly in proportion to the Mexican population explosion after 1975. The personal relationships so important in the U.S.–Mexican political equation began to deteriorate under an apparent Carter–Lopez Portillo confrontation in 1977.

Furthermore, Echeverría's economic policies led to serious weakening of the Mexican economy, causing some illogical bitterness against the U.S. Presumably every chief of state would like to increase exports and reduce imports. However, the Echeverría approach led to massive increases in the balance of payments deficit. Why? Because of this obsession with increasing exports, he began with a major program to increase exports of manufactured goods through development of heavy industry. When this obviously needed large-scale imports of needed heavy capital goods, deficits increased. His policies also caused fright on the part of the Mexican private sector and, apparently, an important capital flow outward from Mexico. Economic decline lasting through 1976 tended to be blamed on the U.S. government, multinationals, etc. The Investment Law of 1973, covered in detail in the chapter on trade and investment, had regulated foreign investment in a manner that at first looked unpromising. Fortunately, however, its application has not restricted foreign capital in Mexico today.

A number of other troubling issues marked the 1974–76 period. Control of drug traffic, despite Mexican government cooperation, caused problems and continues to do so, given the soaring demand for drugs in the U.S. Related was the large number of U.S. citizens imprisoned in Mexico, an issue which remained active until 1977 when a bilateral agreement finally largely resolved it. However, it was widely assumed, in the media as well as in official circles, that the assumption of power by a new Mexican President, Lopez Portillo, on December 1, 1976, and the advent of President Carter in January 1977, would cause the pendulum to swing back to smoother relations. This has not happened, and events from 1977 on have led to pessimism on the part of many trained observers. What went wrong?

Relations of Private Business

First should be noted some specific relationships that seem not only to have survived, but to thrive. The private sector in Mexico, preferring the relative economic caution of Lopez Portillo to the policies of his predecessor, which flew in the face of basic tenets of Mexico's earlier and successful economic policies, has continued to work closely with its counterparts in the U.S. In absolute terms, U.S. trade with Mexico has ballooned and investment has passed the $1 billion a year figure. Though the search for diversification of markets continues, as pushed by the previous Mexican administration, the importance and degree of the bilateral trade relation have continued. In recent attitudes of business groups in Monterrey and Mexico City, there is found a marked eagerness for U.S. investment. Furthermore, among the Mexican private sector there seems to be a willingness and even desire to stress labor-intensive industry for a variety of reasons (including, possibly, mitigating the migration problem). Official policy, to the contrary, has stressed the desire for the most modern type of industry, even if creating fewer jobs.

Therefore, there seems to be a harmony of objectives and an ability to work together on the part of U.S. and Mexican industry and banking which are absent from government-to-government relationships. The powerful business groups in Monterrey have been closely associated with major U.S. corporations for most of the post–World War II period, as have most of the Mexico City business groups, the banking groups of BANAMEX and BANCOMER, and others. The intense desire of the Mexican government to diversify its investment sources in order to prevent "dependence" on the U.S. does not seem to be reflected in attitudes of the private sector. Numerous Mexican leaders in this field have indicated satisfaction at U.S. investment partnership in joint ventures, perhaps in preference to similar experiments with European and Japanese corporations. The latter, of course, are less experienced in working in Mexico. The Mexican private sector has also indicated a preference for dealing with U.S. corporations because they are not so intertwined with their government, as in the case of Japanese business, for example.

In June 1980, a ranking and influential Mexican official indicated in a public statement that he welcomed U.S. investment because he believed it could be concentrated in labor-intensive industry—he was speaking of the Monterrey area—and lead to large increases in employment which would, in turn, reduce pressure on Mexicans to emigrate illegally to the U.S. for work. This, at least, is one attitude which seems to have positive aspects, whether or not it represents official government policy, as evidenced in the Mexican 1976–82 development program.

Along the Border

Before attempting to chronicle current or possible future governmental misunderstandings and difficulties, another exception should be noted. This is the very special situation prevailing on the border. Again, local conditions lead to a different atmosphere from the Washington, D.C.–Mexico City miasma. The interpenetration of the two economies is incontestable and readily visible to all. In the dozen twin cities from Tijuana–San Diego to Matamoros–Brownsville, back-and-forth commerce is a fact. Shopping is where the best buy is; the frontier seems insignificant. Furthermore, given the federal system in the U.S., state administrations have considerable power and ability to administer programs of joint interest on the U.S. side. The Mexican government is far more centralized. It does, however, cooperate fully in maintaining and developing border trade. Given the trade figures involved, it is of vital interest for the commercial elements in both border regions to maintain trade. Statistics show this as being of major significance to both sides.

A special case is the border industry or *maquiladora* program. Basically this program involves U.S. corporations manufacturing parts of their products which have a heavy labor component in Mexico, completing the product, and selling it in the U.S. They can thus take advantage of cheaper labor in Mexico.

Again, without here entering into figures, this is a very positive element in our relations. While the Mexican government has commented relatively little to Washington on this topic, Mexican officials have made clear that this is a helpful and important program, employing as it does some 120,000 workers along the border. An excellent Mexican government movie praising this operation has been prepared. The program, which is outlined in detail in the chapter on trade and investment, likewise is of tangible benefit to the U.S. corporations involved, as they have made clear in public testimony. The border industry program operates because of certain provisions in the U.S. Customs Code. When hearings have been held frequently during the past ten years to determine whether or not to amend these provisions —in effect to terminate the *maquiladora* projects—only the AFL-CIO has publicly favored such action, while a host of private groups in the U.S. has supported the status quo, as well as, very effectively, the American Chamber of Commerce of Mexico and Mexican trade organizations invited to participate. The point to make is that the border industry program is one of the positive factors in the bilateral relationship today and one of the important aspects of the relatively stable and prosperous situation along the border.

The picture of the border situation should not be painted in overly rosy terms. Obviously, there are many conflicts and difficulties. Many of these stem from causes not basically involving the border—except that it is there—like drug trafficking and crossing of illegal immigrants (who, incidentally, come from poorer nonbordering regions). The technical problems resulting from the existence of the border have been made easier over the years by the effective operation of the International Boundary and Waterway Commission, long a model of U.S.–Mexican cooperation at the governmental level. Many organizations, such as the International Good Neighbor Commission, also work in the vineyards of cooperation and achieve results beyond the publicity they generally receive in the nonborder areas of the U.S. Therefore, on balance, the frontier itself should be chalked up as a positive factor in our relations, despite some highly publicized incidents pointing to the contrary.

Current Status: Immigration

Having traced briefly the problems developing during the latter years of the Echeverría period, one comes to the Lopez Portillo administration which, to date, has virtually coincided with the Carter administration. From personal observation, numerous conversations with Mexicans, and from reading declarations of the Mexican President (including the first *Informe* ["State of the Union Message"] on September 1, 1977), I still think that the initial belief was that relations with Washington would be more harmonious than during the Echeverría period. Initial efforts were made, i.e., Lopez Portillo was Carter's first head of state visitor. Bilateral machinery was created in the form of a Consultative Mechanism. Bureaucracy took a step forward in the creation of the position in the Department of State of a coordinator for Mexican affairs. The media assumed that added attention was given to Mexico solely because of its oil resources. However, there seemed to be a more general recognition in official circles that Mexico could no longer be taken for granted and was increasing in importance on a number of fronts, such as in Third World leadership and industrialization.

In trying to determine, sector by sector, what went wrong, perhaps the August 4, 1977, action of President Carter in sending to the Congress the text of proposed legislation governing Mexican illegal workers, without consultation with Mexico, was the first major setback. The natural gas fiasco, which will be discussed later, also clouded the atmosphere early in the two administrations. The issue of immigration in our bilateral relations and its myriad domestic ramifications in both countries are covered extensively in this book by well-known experts in the field. I will limit myself to the effects in overall political relations. The Inter-American Council on Manpower and Development is a small organization which is attempting to undertake normative studies on the *indocumentado* ("illegal alien") issue, perhaps looking to some of the European models for patterns and precedents that might be pertinent. Its very first conclusion is that no approach, governmental or through the private or academic sectors, can succeed unless it is bilateral in nature from the onset. Again viewpoints differ. In the U.S., there is conflict between opponents of Mexican immigration and proponents, to put it blandly. We must realize that in Mexico there is conflict as well as in the U.S. It is understandable that the Mexican government does not choose to take an official position calling for emigration by its citizens to a foreign country. Likewise, it cannot shut its borders to emigration abroad as this would be in violation of the freedom of movement guaranteed by its own constitution. Therefore, there is a basic dichotomy in viewpoints in both countries. Despite some assertions that Mexican immigration to the U.S. is basically a domestic problem, even members of the Senate Judiciary Committee, which has action responsibility for the issue, recognize it as a major issue in foreign relations. (This, of course, is true also to some extent with respect to countries other than Mexico, particularly those of the Caribbean.) Thus, it becomes axiomatic that solutions can only be achieved bilaterally and not unilaterally.

Therefore, the action of submitting the August 1977 proposals on a unilateral basis not only doomed them to failure, but also virtually guaranteed the type of angry Mexican reaction expressed in Washington by then Foreign Secretary Santiago Roel. The contents of the Mexican immigration package became less important than its manner of presentation. In fact, this proposal did contain some positive aspects, and its emphasis on an amnesty for Mexican workers currently in this country was reiterated by the President's Select Commission for Immigration and Refugees (another body created in an effort to cope with the immigration issue on a world-wide basis). From a U.S. domestic political viewpoint the *indocumentado* problem was defused during the 1980 electoral period by the expectation of another U.S. official study.

Whatever may be the current status of the immigration issue, there would be unanimous agreement that it is unsatisfactory and deteriorating. Larger and larger numbers of Mexicans enter the U.S. each year due to both the population explosion and unemployment in Mexico. Therefore, there is no real status quo. Personalities have had little impact on this problem, which is the result of hard economic facts in Mexico coupled with need for the workers in the U.S. It is sufficient to say that, for various reasons, the undocumented alien crisis has worsened since 1977. It is the single most sensitive issue dividing us.

Perhaps we cannot negotiate a settlement for the *indocumentados* now. However, the salinity of the Colorado River, though a more technical issue, seemed impossible to negotiate at one time, without recourse to the International Court of Justice—an action which would have envenomed bilateral relations. Yet it was settled as mentioned. Under current conditions, another conclusion reached is that, for reasons of governmental policies and lack of understanding between the two nations at the official level, the private sector has a vital role to play in financing and supporting studies. Because of internal divisions and for political reasons, there is no consensus in this country. The school that favors major U.S. border control measures, "tortilla curtain" advocates, etc., fortunately seems mostly discredited. These types of actions would cripple the effective working relationship that our two governments require with each other. Those advocating the status quo, as mentioned, advocate something which does not exist and, furthermore, the continuation of practices violating our own laws. The only answer would seem to be in the direction of the guest worker, visiting worker option (not a new *bracero* program).

However, a host of obstacles makes it difficult to proceed. The Mexican government is wary of initiatives. In 1973 a three-point program was presented by Foreign Secretary Rabasa. However, Secretary Kissinger and Mexico's great friend in Congress, Senator Mike Mansfield, estimated this program, with its annual quota feature, could not receive congressional approval. Action, therefore, was aborted. Likewise, the Mexican government has a certain natural reticence on the topic because fundamentally of course it does not, as a long-term policy, favor emigration of its own citizens. Rather, it believes unemployment and the results of the population explosion (the latter now believed diminishing) should be solved by internal development programs. However, tacitly, it can accept the "escape valve" theory in the short term at least. In the U.S., increasing polarization seems to characterize attitudes. There are extremes from the very numerous ranchers and agriculturalists along the border, whose operations depend on Mexican labor, to the Washington-based officials of the AFL-CIO, who hammer away at the job displacement argument in opposing Mexican workers. Thus, inevitably, these internal mechanistic issues have contributed to the cooling of official U.S.–Mexican relations.

Much fundamental study done on both sides of the border, as this book brings out, is in agreement not only on the issues but also on the directions for a solution. Leonel Castillo, former commissioner of immigration, has spoken frequently and eloquently on the need for a guest worker program. Even the President's Select Commission for Immigration and Refugees is undertaking studies on the guest worker approach, but one simply cannot currently predict when action may begin. In the meantime, the problem is indubitably a poison. Mexican media heavily cover incidents of mistreatment at the border. With millions of people involved, they are unavoidable. Nevertheless, the result is a further envenoming of attitudes toward the United States in Mexico City. Statistical tables elsewhere in this volume give the dimensions of the problem. Above all, it has unusual emotional overtones because it involves people, not barrels of oil or boxes of tomatoes. As John Kenneth Galbraith stated, "It is of course outrageous that we seek to turn these people who want so much to work and whose work we so need into some sort of semicriminal class." Others have diametrically opposing views, and we remain at loggerheads, both internally in the U.S. and in our relationships with our neighbor.

Trade: Booming, but with Problems

As late as 1978, Lopez Portillo and the Mexican media were talking of the possibility of a *paquete*—a package settlement of the issues dividing our countries. This approach has now been dropped by the Mexican government, though it still surfaces in the media. On July 20, 1980, the Mexico City daily, *Excelsior*, attacked U.S. Ambassador Julian Nava for attempting, in discussing fishing issues, to dissociate them from other bilateral issues. The *paquete* then included (besides illegal aliens) oil, natural gas, and trade as the principal items. Trade has been an endemic problem. What differentiates Mexican–U.S. trade from other similar relationships throughout the developed and developing world? First is the current volume. Figures are given in detail in the chapter on trade; however, suffice it to say that Mexico is now our third largest trading partner. Traditional trade imbalance has long been a source of Mexican complaint. The Mexican case is based on the large surplus heretofore existing for the U.S. in bilateral commerce. This complaint continues to this day although there are a number of comments to be made.

1. The percentage of exports which Mexico sends to the U.S. has for

many years been higher than the percentage of imports received from this country. This situation still exists.

2. The dollar imbalance is rapidly being rectified by exports of petroleum and natural gas to the U.S. The problems which are reportedly caused to Mexico by currently sending the bulk of her petroleum exports to the U.S. will be discussed later.

3. Even as early as the beginning of the 1970s figures also showed that invisibles largely rectified the commercial imbalance in overall exchanges between the two countries. The invisibles have for most of the postwar period resulted from the excess spent by U.S. tourists in Mexico (supplying about 80 percent of Mexico's total tourist revenues) over amounts—also substantial—spent by Mexican tourists here. The second major source of revenue for Mexico under this heading has been the remittances of Mexican laborers in the U.S. Here again problems are linked—the commercial balance and the illegal alien problem, with the Mexican workers in the U.S. contributing to rectify the trade imbalance.

4. In many of her major trading relationships, the U.S. does not have to take into account emotional and historical animosity. Particularly under the Echeverría administration, the battle cry was economic equality and ending of dependence on the U.S. as a dominant trading partner.

5. As mentioned earlier, the desire of every nation to export more and import less was particularly acute in the Echeverría outlook. Under Lopez Portillo, the approach has been more sophisticated but, of course, is still written into Mexican economic policy. For example, recent large-scale grain imports from the U.S. are not considered by Mexico as a normal transaction to be repeated indefinitely, but rather as an abnormal one to be rectified by agricultural development (whether this view is realistic or not).

6. Though one could conclude that petroleum, as a temporary adjustment factor in previous Mexican balance of payments deficits with the U.S., is helpful, the overall decline in cordiality of official relations has led to continued bitterness on trade issues. Though Mexico has been a protectionist nation—protectionism modified during the Lopez Portillo administration—it has been vocal in attacking U.S. regulations that adversely affect trade, such as antidumping legislation. Again this is a favorite Mexican media topic (just as elements of the

U.S. media have followed a scare campaign against Mexican workers).

United States domination of the Mexican market will decline, although in dollar terms it will continue to increase. While U.S. trade
policy since the Cordell Hull era has officially been dedicated to free
trade—and most of the few trade agreements finally concluded in the
Roosevelt period were with Latin America—free traders are presently
in difficulties, especially with regard to Japan. Concerning Mexico,
there is a feeling among some students that the decade of the 1980s
will require a fundamental reassessment of Mexican commercial policy. The antiprotectionist measures of President Lopez Portillo indicate an awareness of this, and the trend toward relaxing trade barriers
in Mexican official doctrine may continue. However, as of now, there
are U.S. critics who seriously question whether Mexico can become a
major exporter of industrial goods, as the 1976–82 development plan
calls for, and concurrently maintain a structure of protection that is
more suitable to a nation less further advanced in the development
scale. Thus, to conclude, snarls between trading partners are inevita-
ble the world over—see U.S. and Japan. However, in the U.S.–Mexican
case, because of historical factors, the strong desire of Mexico for "economic independence," and a tendency to personalize blame in these
disputes, commercial activity has been particularly politicized and has
become a tenser issue in official relations. Though annual negotiations
on such issues as cotton textile quotas and periodic revisions of the air
route agreement are always finally concluded, there is usually long and
somewhat acrimonious debate. To put it in perspective, though, we
can recall that air route negotiations between the U.S. and Ireland
seemed almost eternal. Nevertheless, trade will remain a major factor
in any U.S.–Mexican *paquete.*

Role of Mexican Petroleum

Turning to the energy question, Mexican oil has been a favorite
for media speculation about U.S. relations with Mexico. Will the old
term "special relationship" be revived in the context of Mexican petroleum exports? Will a deal be struck to permit Mexican workers free
access to U.S. job markets in exchange for favorable oil prices? Will
Mexico reduce U.S. dependence on Middle East oil? Since we are
neighbors, and transportation naturally costs less from Mexico to the
U.S. than from the Persian Gulf, won't Mexico's oil naturally gravi-

tate here? The answer to all of these questions is probably "no." Mexicans are tired of meaningless talk about a "special relationship" that consists only of exceptions to granting anything "special" to Mexico when a case arises. Why would Mexico establish a particularly favorable oil export structure for the U.S. when it feels the U.S. has failed to grant Mexico such terms in connection with items it wishes to send here on a regular large-scale basis (tomatoes, for example)? There is no substance to press speculation that a "cheaper oil in exchange for accepting Mexican workers" deal is under consideration. This idea is fraught with difficulties and would doubtless sink in the congressional swamp, simply a nonstarter. It is not in the cards from the Mexican viewpoint either.

Mexican oil export figures are given elsewhere in this book. They show that since exports began in 1976, the bulk has come to the U.S. However, the official Mexican position (also reflected elsewhere in this book) is that, as in every other category of economic activity, Mexico seeks diversification of markets and avoidance of dependence on the U.S., a recurrent theme. Therefore, far from seeking to consolidate or increase exports to the U.S., Mexico is anxious to increase sales to other customers. Spain and Israel are already proving to be good markets, while Japan is a natural potential customer of major significance. Therefore, the relationship of U.S. dependence on Middle East crude and imports from other OPEC nations (of which Mexico is, of course, not one) to Mexico's oil program is coincidental. Furthermore, conservative Mexican extraction policy (at least to date) does not promise any major substitution for present oil import sources.

To the argument that, in the interest of overall conservation and prevention of unnecessary price increases, it is more efficient for Mexico to sell oil to the U.S., the Mexican reply is that it sells oil at a fixed price in a fixed place. This factor is, thus, basically irrelevant to Mexico. Furthermore, Mexican oil price is dictated by domestic economic considerations. It is well within the upper OPEC range and above, for example, Saudi Arabia. There is a certain comforting geostrategic angle to having Mexico's large oil resources across the border and not halfway around the world. The value of this is simply not calculable now. Whatever may be the surface impressions, Mexican oil is not a built-in bargain for the U.S. It will be priced and marketed at the levels best suited to Mexico's view of its own developmental interests. In the long term, oil revenues may lead to improving the basic structural maladjustments of the Mexican economy, for instance, in the rural sector. This would lead to a strengthening and improvement of the economy which would be in the interest of both countries.

What the Mexican government will do with its oil revenues is obviously of primary importance. President Lopez Portillo, in his 1978 *Informe* and elsewhere, has indicated three primary areas of concentration. The first is continued research for petroleum which is being pursued vigorously with proven resources now announced at 50 billion barrels. Probable and potential reserves are at 150 billion barrels. The second objective is to undertake job training programs. The third is to improve radically conditions in rural areas. The latter two points are of major significance and how these programs unfold will be vital.

The Natural Gas Fiasco

In any discussion of oil, natural gas also must be mentioned. An agreement on natural gas led to a major fiasco in U.S.–Mexican relations. As was widely covered in the press, six U.S. corporations had made an agreement with PEMEX, the Mexican state petroleum agency, for construction of a major pipeline and the purchase of 2 billion cubic feet of natural gas at a price of \$2.40 per thousand cubic feet. Under pressure from then Secretary of Energy James Schlesinger, the corporations were forced to cancel the deal. This led to one of the major disillusionments of President Lopez Portillo with the Carter administration. The rationale used by the U.S. Department of Energy was that the Mexican price was higher than the Canadian at the juncture and that the escalator clause was undesirable. But the results were a political disaster. Finally, recently a much smaller deal was negotiated for the purchase of 300 million cubic feet of Mexican gas. Both the Mexican and Canadian prices are now, incidentally, well over \$4.00 per thousand cubic feet. Thus, the result was not only that we received much less gas at a much higher price at a much later date, but also that the adverse political fallout was being felt long after the event.

Tourism

Tourism is overall a positive factor in the U.S.–Mexican equation. As mentioned, the balance is heavily in Mexico's favor. Expansion of tourist facilities remains Mexican government policy. The U.S.

and Canada supply almost all of the tourists, 80 percent of tourist expenditures coming from the U.S. Obviously, there are strains and incidents resulting from the large number of people involved, and certain aspects of Mexico lead to considerable grumbling on occasions. However, U.S. citizens seem to consider Mexico basically a good tourist locale. Mexico also has benefited from the decline of the dollar vis-à-vis European currencies, making European tourist destinations expensive for Americans. In this instance, the Mexican "devaluation" of 1976, or, more accurately, the floating of the peso, has proved advantageous as the peso settled almost immediately at a stable rate of about 22.50 pesos to the dollar from the earlier 12.50. Thus Mexico has remained relatively in an advantageous position to obtain the tourist dollar.

Tourism has not played a major role in the political relationship of the two countries, perhaps by the definition of a tourist. The Consultative Mechanism and the Quadripartite Commission in New York (a mixed business and government group of the representing two countries) have addressed themselves to increasing tourism through such mechanisms as possible package tours to the two countries, but fundamentally this matter is in the hands of the travel agencies.

GATT: Mexico Says "No"

With regard to multilateral economic agencies, U.S.–Mexican relations of course took one more on the chin in the Mexican decision not to join the General Agreement on Tariffs and Trade (GATT). Mexico received extensive trade benefits negotiated with the U.S. in advance, but the decision announced by Lopez Portillo seems to have had political origins. Extensive coverage of the GATT episode in the Mexico City press persisted in innuendos tarring the GATT organization as U.S.–dominated. Mexican adherence thereto thus somehow continued a pattern of dependence. Perhaps it is merely a factor of the greater U.S. influence in all international organisms because of its size and economic weight. In any event, Mexico did not join, though other major developing nations such as Brazil are members.

Mexico Buys Grain, Sells Tomatoes

Finally, during 1980 some of the adverse conditions were mitigated by the Mexican purchase of over 10 million tons of U.S. grains.

Obviously there existed a need in Mexico following two years of drought and increasing demand resulting from population increase. The timing, however, was fortuitous. The largest individual sale followed closely after President Carter had banned additional grain shipments to the Soviet Union following the invasion of Afghanistan, thus creating unexpected availabilities here. There is some evidence to support the thesis that President Lopez Portillo did wish to improve relations somewhat following a series of episodes which will be mentioned shortly. Whatever the reason, the size and timing of Mexican purchases were well-received in Washington.

Again, understandably, the official Mexican position is that these purchases are an emergency measure not automatically to be repeated. Still, when one considers such things as official birth rate figures of 3.4 percent annual increase until very recently, Mexican crop conditions, and the emphasis on industrial growth, it would seem that a Mexican market for large quantities of U.S. grains would exist for some time. As a counterpart, the Mexicans would expect a more open market and a more regularized situation with regard to exports of their winter fruits and vegetables, which form an important part of the export economy of Pacific Coast states such as Sinaloa. The annual "tomato war" has thus far been settled each year, circumventing the opposition of Florida tomato growers to Mexican imports. However, annually, with the beginning of the Mexican exporting season in January, there is a press campaign in both nations that unfailingly is characterized by hostility.

North American Common Market

Another irritant is the so-called North American Common Market, the basic feasibility of which has not even been studied, much less formally presented to anyone. This surfaced in the presidential campaign of Governor Jerry Brown of California. It was originally the subject of an article by an investment banking house in New York. The splendid phrase never seemed to have had substance. How it would operate is undetermined. Have those who talk of this studied the Treaty of Rome? The degree of similarity to the European model envisaged is unknown. Obviously a sensible first step would be a study by academic experts of the three nations involved. Instead, instant speculation only led immediately to denunciations in the Mexican press of this as another Yankee plot to keep Mexico subjugated. The reasoning was that the economic disparity of the U.S. and the other two members would lead to U.S. dominance. Not only that, but it was also put forth that this was somehow a means of guaranteeing Mexican oil exports to the U.S.

Probably this was an "in-good-faith" idea that became prematurely public before the pros and cons had been studied or even considered. Again, whatever might be the possibility of such an idea, or what form it would take—and it does seem a long way from reality—the premature appearance of the North American Common Market as a possible policy for three nations led to its denunciation in Mexico and has probably eliminated it for the foreseeable future. Government agencies in Washington, incidentally, have never become officially involved. Nor have they indicated this represented U.S. official thinking, presumably on the correct grounds that any such stand would be premature. Lopez Portillo declared to the Canadian Parliament in May of 1980 that "proposals [along this line] are incompatible with the objectives of Mexico's social and economic development, in view of the great difference between the development levels of the three countries." In the same speech, he announced an agreement to sell fifty thousand barrels of oil a day to Canada in exchange for Canadian assistance in Mexican development, presumably as a minideclaration of independence.

Other Irritants on Both Sides

The *paquete* problems discussed above—immigration, trade, oil, natural gas—are precisely those that are most resistant to solution. As Professor Peter Smith points out in *Mexico: A Quest for a U.S. Policy* (1980), the illusion persists that somehow it is possible, given good will, for a bunch of negotiators to sit down and settle these matters. I agree that it is not. They will persist. Therefore, as mentioned, perhaps the best we can do is massage them, keep them before us, and seize opportunities that might occasionally arise over the coming years to lessen their ability to disturb U.S.–Mexican relations.

If these are endemic problems that somehow are viewed with greater emotion now than previously, what added irritants have arisen to make relations generally worse now than ten years ago? Other than the increase of Mexican desire for an independent stance and U.S. "respect,"

to use Lopez Portillo's favorite word, a series of almost extraneous incidents occurred during the Carter–Lopez Portillo periods in office.
These seem of a tit-for-tat nature. The disasters of the Carter visit to
Mexico City have been widely publicized in both countries. President
Carter's unfortunate remarks were seized upon by the media. However
insubstantial this incident was, it has remained on the tip of the
tongue, particularly in Mexico City. It is utilized as symbolic of U.S.
lack of understanding of Mexico, insensitivity, and disrespect. The
Mexican reaction was deep, and the most thoughtful and moderate
Mexicans have indicated their dismay. Anti-American elements of
various stripes have had a field day. Whatever else may have been discussed during the visit, the public souvenir that remains is of a single
remark. Even earlier, Lopez Portillo had been unhappy with his initial
White House reception.

Talks between the two Presidents in Washington likewise led to certain acrimony. Frankly, U.S. ambassadorial appointments also caused
controversy and unhappiness in the Mexican press. One ambassador
was criticized because he did not speak Spanish, and his successor, it
could almost be said, for precisely the opposite reason. This is a super-
ficial reaction to Mexican attitudes of course. Mexicans realize that
ambassadorial appointments are the prerogative of the sending state.
Nevertheless, they feel that, especially when the U.S. talks of a "special
relationship," their attitudes on this subject might be taken into account. The U.S. ambassador in Mexico City, as in Ottawa, has traditionally had a position of some importance. Therefore, the Mexicans,
in broad perspective, do wish to have an incumbent who is sympathetic
to, and understanding of, their positions and feelings. Furthermore,
they wish to have broad communication with the U.S. Embassy and to
have U.S. representatives who have the maximum possible knowledge
not only of their politics and history, but also of their language and
culture. Thus, while in no way seeking to judge the merits of the Mexican attitude, it can be concluded that during the Carter administration
this particular issue, which had been dormant for many years, rose
again. Every student will recall the profound distaste of Mexicans for
the interventionist activities of one U.S. ambassador during the Madero
period, culminating in the so-called "Pact of the Embassy" in 1913.
While recent appointees are not accused of interference in internal
affairs, nevertheless, for varying reasons, Mexican media reactions
have been unfavorable to the appointments. With regard to Ambassa-

dor Nava, there appears to be no personal animus whatever. Rather, there is a feeling that the appointment was made in Washington for domestic political reasons and that Mexico was sort of a second choice assignment. All of this feeds the lack of respect theme and causes controversy that has little substance.

During a reading of the Mexico City press in March and April of 1980, all of the sore spots previously mentioned were rubbed some more. In addition, there were other complaints. For example, there were complaints against the 1976 Tax Reform Act, which limits tax exemption privileges for conventions held abroad by U.S. groups. Although this measure has world-wide applicability, Mexico, a convention favorite because of proximity and for other reasons, is primarily affected. Mexican reaction was similar in the case of the 10 percent duty surcharge which was levied by Secretary of the Treasury John Connally in 1972. While this affected all nations, Mexico and Canada were particularly incensed, being neighbors supposedly with "special relationships." Furthermore, even more persistent, the U.S. had then a healthy trade surplus with Mexico. Visa requirements for Mexicans to visit the U.S. as tourists or on business surface as an issue periodically. A thorn to Mexico is the fact that businessmen in France, for instance, can obtain the necessary visa for the U.S. by mail, while in Mexico, time-consuming visits to the U.S. Embassy are required for a visa for business purposes. One could dwell on countless relatively minor issues of this nature. The important fact, however, is that added together they prejudice the objective of a cordial and useful working relationship between the two governments.

As a result of the foregoing issues in which the U.S. had acted in a way designed to upset Mexican feelings, President Lopez Portillo more recently has commenced a series of actions and declarations which have, in turn, injured feelings in Washington. The point had been reached by 1980 where some Washington-based journalists were saying that Mexico is one of the least popular foreign countries with the White House. Perhaps an exaggeration, but there is little reason to doubt that Lopez Portillo's statements, whether viewed in Mexico as concerted actions or not, have further exacerbated relations. This in turn led to reactions of annoyance in Washington and a belief that Mexico is deliberately seeking to distance itself economically and politically from the U.S.

Washington had been accustomed to the Third World rhetoric

emanating from Mexico City in the Echeverría period. At that time, a more aggressive friendship with Cuba developed, though not with the Soviet Union. Through such steps as the Charter of Rights and Duties of Nations, mentioned at the beginning of this chapter, Mexico tried to assume a mantle of Third World leadership. Despite Mexican industrialization and continued emphasis on production of heavy capital goods, etc., for political purposes Mexico placed herself in the Third World category like a Haiti or a Honduras. This rhetoric consisted of almost continual proposals that the most developed countries, especially the U.S., contribute a larger share of their gross national product to needs of developing countries. Though this was disconcerting to Washington, it likewise reflected the views of many U.S. developmental economists.

Episodes of the first half of 1980 appeared more provocative to those studying Mexican affairs in the U.S., although their full intention is perhaps not known. The most publicized was the "Shah of Iran affair." All will recall the refusal of the Mexican government to receive the Shah back from New York where he had gone from Cuernavaca for medical treatment. Mention of the rationale for this refusal may be pertinent, though the exact sequence of events might still be murky to the public. The statement issued by Lopez Portillo at the time stated that acceptance of the Shah for a second time might prejudice Mexico's policy for nonalignment and, presumably, her position of influence and leadership among developing countries. Why this was not relevant earlier is not entirely clear. The reaction in Washington was openly sour for a number of reasons. First, the U.S. had assisted in the evacuation of the Mexican Embassy from Tehran as a backdrop for Mexico's accepting the Shah a second time. Second, the decision was a last-minute one. Until very late, Washington had reason to believe, based on assurances, that return would be permitted. Third, of course, the departure of the Shah from Cuernavaca to New York had precipitated the hostage crisis, which had been predicted in the event the former ruler came to this country. Washington was therefore in a particularly bitter mood, though Mexico could hardly be blamed for any responsibility in the hostage tragedy.

Attacks on Lopez Portillo for failing to welcome the Shah back merely further annoyed Mexico City, and other incidents followed. The President of Mexico made a statement to the effect that the United States had committed an error in freezing Iranian assets. This, bluntly, was felt in U.S. government circles to be none of his business. The confrontation continued when Mexico made a statement that the dollar might no longer be a satisfactory or reliable currency on which to base petroleum transactions and called for its replacement by another base, such as the special drawing rights. Again, the U.S. reaction was one of annoyance and a feeling that the Mexican statement was gratuitous. Although the Mexican peso had been dissociated from the dollar at the time of the 1976 devaluation, in fact it had remained closely related to the dollar at a stable rate. So the Mexican statement seemed unnecessary, especially as the major U.S. oil suppliers in OPEC, such as Saudi Arabia and Nigeria, had not raised this issue. In New York, a Mexican statement at the time of the vote on Iranian sanctions in the U.N. led to further anger in the White House. Mexico was thought to be, judging from the declaration's language, deliberately opposing the U.S. purely for the sake of ruffling waters.

Thus in the winter and spring of 1980, there was an incontestable deterioration of relations. As mentioned above, large and well-timed Mexican grain purchases have alleviated matters somewhat. Later, on June 24, 1980, though, Lopez Portillo gave an interview to the directors of the Associated Press which again listed a bill of complaints against U.S. policies and attitudes under the general heading of "lack of respect" by the U.S. for its neighbor. During the U.S. electoral campaign, Mexican relations remained somewhat in limbo. Expert observers in both countries concur that there has been a deterioration, and it seriously worries many.

The Personal Equation

An element adding to the complexity was the apparent incompatibility from 1977 through 1980 of the two heads of state. An examination of the precise reason for the chemical failure of this relationship is perhaps irrelevant, probably impossible. Nevertheless, all observers comment on this point. Those who saw the two together are convinced of a lack of understanding that became a near phobia. This is unfortunate, particularly because the nature of U.S. ties with both Mexico and Canada has led to unusually frequent contact at the head of state level, beginning in World War II. In the period 1969–74, for example, there were six summit meetings. This has normally been a positive element in the bilateral relation. While the meetings were not always earthshaking, they represented a positive aspect of the relationship. Frequently they gave an impetus to settling some controversy. Heads of state love to make announcements of major specific settlements and agreements when they meet, so the bureaucrat is always under pressure to furnish some meat for these repasts. Without taking space here to analyze presidential meetings from Franklin D. Roosevelt and Alvia Camacho through 1976, most observers would concur that the total impact had been very positive as a factor in strengthened U.S.–Mexican relations. While there were fairly numerous "ho-hum" meetings, there were also spectacular public successes, such as those in Mexico of President Truman (unexpected at the time) and President Kennedy.

Therefore, the unraveling of the personal tie has added to the difficulties. The thesis that the immigration issue, for instance, cannot now be settled by negotiators seems correct. Nor can trade problems be amicably terminated to everyone's satisfaction. Nevertheless it does seem necessary to flag the incompatibility on a personal level of the two Presidents as an unnecessary added handicap.

Mexican-Americans

A factor unique in the U.S.–Mexican relationship is the existence of very large and growing numbers of U.S. citizens of Mexican origin. It is not the purpose of this article to examine the sociological connotations of this major phenomenon, but to mention briefly how it might be interpreted as affecting attitudes of the U.S. and Mexican governments on the issues separating us. Mexican government policy has logically been not to take positions publicly on problems facing Mexican-Americans, or Chicanos, in the U.S. Those who are U.S. citizens are obviously outside Mexican government sovereignty or protection.

An example of this Mexican attitude occurred in San Antonio in 1972 when a group of Chicano activists from Crystal City, Texas, asked for an interview with President Echeverría, who was on an official tour of the United States. Echeverría initially refused to see the group but later relented. After permitting them to pour out a long list of grievances of supposed discrimination against Mexican-Americans in this country, Echeverría told them, also at length and emphatically, that they had no claims to assistance from the Mexican authorities. He made the point that Mexico had not exiled these people, that they had left their country voluntarily, and, indeed, that he considered them somewhat of a national embarrassment. He concluded with a restatement of his position: that their problems, as U.S. citizens, were totally outside his competence. Although this position was not well received by the Mexican-Americans involved, it was clear.

In Mexico City, problems of Mexican-Americans are covered in the media but without particular emphasis. Groups of Mexican-American visiting students and others receive low-key publicity. Sympathy is reserved for the *indocumentados* whose troubles are covered in detail. An incident in February 1980, in which a small Mexican child was killed in a border area, was heavily reported in the press and on television. At a meeting on U.S.–Mexican relations of the World Affairs Council of San Diego in March 1980, the prominent Mexican immigration expert, Professor Jorge Bustamente, outlined how this incident, and others which occurred, colored the U.S.–Mexican relationship. Bustamente pointed out that human tragedy of this nature affected popular outlook in Mexico more than barrels of statistics about Mexican migrants.

However, the progress of the U.S. citizens of Mexican origin in this country inevitably is followed in Mexico. President Lopez Portillo received a group of Mexican-Americans in New York. Apparently he was enough concerned by their representations to mention their expressed plight in Washington, where his taking up their cause was not well received. This was followed up by the creation of a Mexican liaison group for Mexican-Americans. Again, although outside the scope of this chapter, the question of the net effect of the existence of millions of U.S. citizens of Mexican origin on the bilateral relationship is fascinating, if not entirely clear. The primary interest of this group in the U.S. has seemed to be to make social and economic progress within the framework of the American society. For instance, the position of Cesar Chavez and his organization with regard to illegal Mexican workers has been typical. It has vacillated between opposition, on the grounds that large numbers of additional Mexican workers might prejudice the successes of his own union labor (presumably mostly U.S. citizens) and support for his "fellow Mexicans." The attitude has never been finalized but is symptomatic of the schizophrenia on the illegal alien problem on the part of Mexican-Americans, who are naturally concerned firstly with their own progress in the society to which they now belong.

Mexican media, such as the influential daily *Excelsior,* have considered generally that U.S. citizens of Mexican origin probably were discriminated against in terms of job opportunities. Chicano groups from areas such as Los Angeles, who have visited Mexico City and complained of the absence of sufficient Spanish-language educational opportunities in the U.S., have received fairly wide and generally sympathetic coverage in *Excelsior.* The theme of persecution of Mexican immigrant workers and an alleged inferior status for Mexican-Americans has also surfaced from time to time in publications such as the anti–U.S. weekly *Siempre.* However, Mexican government concern has been centered on Mexican citizens who enter the U.S. to work without documentation, their treatment and their plight.

Mexicans, of course, have widely differing views on their excompatriots who are now U.S. citizens. Perhaps, in border regions, the relations are closer and more harmonious. In Mexico City, a certain condescension is noted. An attitude of superiority is sometimes felt—a feeling that those who left were not members of the governing elites. Conversely, many sociologists believe that those who are leaving now to work in the U.S. from mostly rural areas are among the most energetic and ambitious elements who, on their return, could form local elites. Some of the Mexican-Americans, of course, are the descendants of those residing in territories that were taken over by the United States after the Treaty of Guadalupe-Hidalgo in 1848, and thus citizens of the U.S. for well over a century.

How do the Mexican-Americans feel about U.S.–Mexican relations? Doubtless they are influenced by generally the same considerations as other segments of the U.S. population. Obviously there is great interest in Mexican relations on their part, but indeed Mexico is generally occupying a more important place in everyone's mind. The best-known American scholars of Mexico are persons such as John Womak of Harvard and not necessarily Mexican-Americans. Obviously this subject can be better commented on by individuals with direct knowledge. There is no evidence in Washington of a Mexican-American lobby on behalf of Mexican government positions on economic or other issues. Indeed, the pressures that exist for more favorable treatment of Mexican exports to the U.S. come primarily from business groups with interests in Mexico, represented by the American Chamber of Commerce of Mexico, whose nearly three thousand members favor such action.

In late June 1980, at a meeting of the governors of the U.S. and Mexican border states in Ciudad Juárez, Mexico, the positions taken by the U.S. governors were determined, naturally, by their view of the overall interests of their states in more amicable and effective working relations with Mexico. They did not espouse any specific Mexican-American causes. The governors, particularly Governor William Clements of Texas, pleaded hard for close ties between the two central governments that would parallel those between the border states. The U.S. governors, however, were representing all of their constituents. There does not appear to be a lobby of millions of Mexican-Americans advocating more favorable attitudes toward Mexico. Are they less concerned than Irish-Americans, for instance, about developments in their exhomeland? One cannot determine perhaps, but this is obviously a question of interest.

Mexico City has had rather cynical reactions to the announcements of Presidents Nixon and Carter about a greater role for Mexican-Americans in the United States and greater participation in government appointments. The reaction noted was that the naming of some Mexican-Americans to government jobs does not represent a fundamental change. On the other side, tourism to such places as Acapulco and other resorts does not seem to attract Mexican-Americans to any special degree. Thus, while the large Mexican-American population in this country is indubitably a factor to be studied and considered in this total picture, there is no evidence that it seeks to play an advocacy role in either U.S. or Mexican policies, which are dictated by other factors, primarily economic.

A Peek at the Future

Having cataloged a series of woes and some positive points, one must mention prospects for the future. It is clear that the major outstanding issues—immigration, petroleum, and a host of trade problems—are simply not susceptible to being negotiated under current conditions. U.S. policy is currently paralyzed and no major initiatives can be expected for a long time. Decisive developments in the *indocumentado* issue depend on studies taking into account fundamental divergencies in U.S. and Mexican attitudes on the issue and utilizing precedents for successful immigrant worker programs such as have taken place in western Europe. Trade problems, insofar as the U.S. is concerned, depend primarily on congressional action, in turn reflecting the local interest of constituents in controlling Mexican imports of agricultural and manufactured goods. The role of petroleum in the relationship is subject to the factors mentioned earlier. All of these are long-term problems.

If the major issues are unlikely to achieve progress (most likely at least until 1982), what can be done about more general atmospherics, at least to prevent further deterioration? The major Mexican watchword seems to be "respect." Misunderstandings have already been chronicled. Is the situation hopeless? No. Beyond and behind some apparently harsh Mexican public positions, there is almost undoubtedly room for maneuver. On immigration, a jointly developed guest worker program does not seem unacceptable to the Mexicans, according to sources in Mexico City. It would serve certain short- and medium-term objectives of official Mexican policy. However, as indicated, a Mexican initiative is unlikely because of past rebuffs. Given dissension between Washington and Mexico City, progress may be currently blocked, but development of a program could at least be undertaken by nongovernmental elements in the two countries. The trade war will doubtless struggle on, but, as a minimum, official groups charged with responsibility in Washington should prevent any nibbling away at the present situation where Mexican markets in this country do remain substantially open.

A hopeful note was struck at the governors' meeting mentioned earlier (incidentally, the first of its kind). The six governors from the Mexican states bordering on the U.S. were the hosts, excellent and cordial hosts indeed. In view of the strong centralization of the Mexican government, the enthusiastic participation of the Mexican governors in this meeting not only had the blessing of President Lopez Portillo but also his active interest. Doubtless, too, the Mexican participants had been briefed at the highest level. The forthcoming and cooperative positions they took on numerous issues from immigration to border industries and cultural relations must have had the support of the central government. Conceivably, the Mexican government was using this forum to convey more forthcoming attitudes on current problems than has been the case in its interchanges with Washington.

In any event, it would seem to show a welcome Mexican flexibility.

The future of personality problems is of course unpredictable. They will eventually probably dissipate, and the warmer cordiality of an earlier era can return. This is important in connection with the unnecessary irritants of little substance that have been mentioned. It has been stated almost *ad nauseum* that the U.S. has failed to realize Mexico's new place in the world, gained by her industrialization and oil resources. Nevertheless, this Mexican complaint remains a factor, as does the importance of the decline of the overall position of the U.S. in the world.

Mexico has vigorously supported the present Nicaraguan government. Although the executive branch of the U.S. government has also favored assistance to Nicaragua, Mexico has taken a position of even stronger support. Indeed, Mexico has pointed to the Sandinista regime as a model for its Central American neighbors. Likewise, Mexico's policy toward Chile has been much more vociferous than that of the U.S. in spite of Washington's coldness toward the Pinochet government since the assassination of former Chilean Foreign Minister Letelier. These differences of approach are somewhat more marked than previously and reflect Mexican "independence."

We can expect more Mexican initiatives in foreign policy, especially in this hemisphere. This should not necessarily be troubling, and Washington indeed has reacted with public equanimity to date. Specifically, of course, a moratorium on punishing public statements would be helpful. This cannot be negotiated because it is a matter of atmosphere. However, annoyed reactions to statements such as that of Lopez Portillo's with regard to the stability of the dollar will continue in this country. Technical issues will continue to be debated in the Consultative Mechanism and in normal diplomatic interchange. Issues which have to be arranged will be.

In conclusion, therefore, perhaps the best prospects are to retreat from current issues, prevent further deterioration, eschew harmful and unnecessary verbiage, and reexamine fundamentals. The cardinal point in U.S. policy toward Mexico has not varied in many years. It is simply to establish and preserve a cordial and effective working relationship, given the two thousand miles of border we share, the increasing importance of our trading partnership, and the strategic concurrence of our interests. Mexican policy toward us would seem to share the same considerations and to have the same objectives.

Leaving aside any sentimental aspects of the ties between us, Mexico, with minimal defense forces, equipment, and expenditures, tacitly depends on the U.S. in the strategic field. Concurrently, the U.S. finds it important to have a friendly, peaceful, and stable Mexico on its boundary. One could almost conclude that we are condemned to live together. This argues for making the best of it—not the opposite, as it would seem is currently happening.

With the basic need for a useful relation generally accepted, we would be better advised to avoid exacerbating day-to-day conditions to such a point they might threaten the long-term fundamentals. Maybe all that can be done is to accept the basics, continue to move forward when possible on technical issues, and wait for another day. The major issues will not disappear, and their settlement may take the rest of the decade. Trade will never be regulated to everyone's satisfaction. However, if the seemingly intransigent border problem was finally settled with the 1963 and 1970 treaties, there is certainly hope that the two neighbors, both mature powers, can eventually settle their differences. With regard to the new bitterness of the past few years, time may heal these new wounds, personalities will change, and eventually the cordiality of the 1940 to 1974 era could return.

Juan Eibenschutz *

2

Energy Issues in Mexico

Mexico has been a fortunate country insofar as energy resources are concerned. During the 1920s, when its oil was still being exploited by foreign companies, Mexico played a major exporting role, with its share of the international market reaching a level of 200,000 barrels daily in 1922.

The country's energy endowment contributed to the development of the economies of countries receiving Mexican oil in those days, but it also led to the creation of a national awareness of energy's strategic value. During the revolutionary period, the justice of the exploitation of nonrenewable resources by foreign companies was questioned; the 1917 Constitution specified that the nation had exclusive ownership of hydrocarbons, and later, once the national political situation had been stabilized, the decision to nationalize the oil industry was reached in 1938.

The political repercussions of this national decision are widely known. For the purposes of this chapter, it is interesting to mention that that was the world's first nationalization of a petroleum industry.

---

* Translated by Frances Horning Barraclough.

JUAN EIBENSCHUTZ *is coordinator of the Management and Planning Committee of the Mexican Federal Electricity Commission. Formerly, he was the executive secretary of the Energy Commission. Mr. Eibenschutz has written and lectured extensively on petroleum and energy, and has participated in several international energy studies. He directs the Mexican National Committee of the World Energy Conference.*

With that act the largest national industry was originated, thus developing an institution that has been the answer to the country's hopes by becoming an integrated petroleum industry, as highly complex as any now existing in the world.

Oil, however, is not the only energy source at the country's disposal. The origins of oil production and its availability served to create an awareness of energy's importance to the nation's functioning and development. The Constitution, besides giving the nation ownership rights over energy resources, clearly establishes the federation's exclusive right to exploit all sources of energy in order to meet the public energy demand.

Until a few years ago, the governmental entities responsible for meeting demands for various kinds of energy were operating in a system of relative independence, since control over plans and programs was held by the government ministries responsible for the budget. In 1973 the Comisión de Energeticos ("Energy Resources Commission") was set up, becoming in fact a precedent for the current administrative reform that gives the responsibility for energy policy and coordination to the Secretaría de Patrimonio y Fomento Industrial ("Ministry of National Wealth and Development").

The fundamental responsibility of the entities making up the energy sector—Petroleos Mexicanos, Comisión Federal de Electricidad, Comisión Nacional de Energía Atómica, and the coal industries—is to meet the national demand in order to guarantee the operation of the industry and of the different energy-demanding sectors, thereby insuring that the country in general will have possibilities for growth.

As a result of the oil discoveries at the beginning of the 1970s, which had already been indicated several decades before, energy resources acquired a new dimension in the context of national policy. The original focus was that Mexico had sufficient resources to meet its own needs and could rely on having the fuel base needed for a reasonable development, compatible with population and economic growth. The possibility of exporting energy made financial self-determination possible, and with it the setting of more ambitious goals. But at the same time it created a need for thinking about the effects export-derived financial resources could have on the country.

In this chapter I shall attempt to cover, on the one hand, the energy resources and production plans available to the country and, on the other, the general philosophy with which production plans and national energy export levels are set.

Energy Resources

HYDROCARBONS

The preponderance of hydrocarbons in the Mexican energy balance is well known. At this writing there are total oil and gas reserves of 50 billion barrels of crude oil equivalent. Taking into account, on the one hand, the estimates of potential reserves and, on the other, geological analyses, it is reasonable to state that Mexico has one of the world's most important oil potentials.

Fig. 1. Proven reserves of hydrocarbons

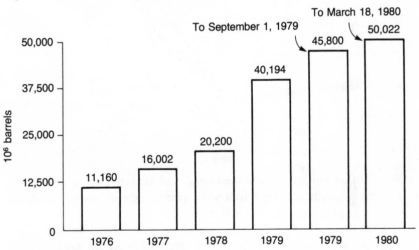

There are 2.3 million barrels of petroleum and gas liquids, in addition to 3,500 million cubic feet of natural gas, produced daily. These production levels were reached quite rapidly if one realizes that at the end of 1976 daily production was running at about 950,000 barrels of crude and liquid and approximately 2,000 million cubic feet of natural gas.

As for reserves, it is fitting to point out that the methodology for

Fig. 2. Relation of reserves to production of hydrocarbons

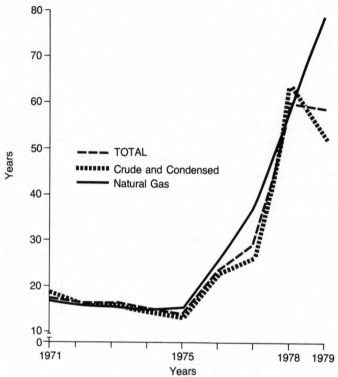

their evaluation has been modernized and that the utilization of exploratory results obtained in recent years made it possible to reach the levels noted in preceding paragraphs.

The most important fields are found in the southeastern part of the country, in the states of Tabasco, Veracruz, Chiapas, the Gulf of Campeche, and in the Chicontepec zone; in the northern part of the state of Veracruz and the state of Tamaulipas; and in the northwestern region of the country in the states of Tamaulipas, part of Nuevo León, and Coahuila.

There are other regions with theoretically important possibilities of containing hydrocarbons on the west coast as well as in the middle of the country and in the highlands. Nevertheless, it is particularly in the eastern region that already located reserves have made it possible to reach present production levels, and in this respect it is important to point out that the Campeche offshore zone is where the most spectacular production developments have occurred, with a level of more than 800,000 barrels daily being attained by the middle of 1980.

COAL

The country's coal-bearing potential, according to information thus far available, is relatively low, as reserves which have been positively accounted for until now come to about 2 billion tons which, although important compared to present production, do not allow Mexico to count on this resource as very significant for the country's future energy balance. Possibly there is still insufficient information available, and as exploratory work proceeds, more important volumes of coal may be discovered.

HYDROELECTRIC ENERGY

It has been estimated that Mexico has the potential to produce about 120 tetrawatt-hours (TWh) per year, which could substitute for approximately half a million barrels daily of fuel oil. Hydroelectric production is about 18 TWh annually, and it is estimated that in the year 2000 it will be possible to develop enough facilities to produce some 80 TWh per year, which at that date could replace about 300,-000 barrels of fuel oil daily.

The most important hydroelectric sites are located on the Grijalva, Usumacinta, and Balsas rivers, while other lower power potential sites exist in different watersheds throughout the country.

URANIUM

Reserves of this mineral that have been discovered and quantified amount to some ten thousand tons, which would be enough to satisfy —for approximately thirty years—the demands of the first nuclear power plant, presently under construction.

In the case of this energy resource, geological indications seem to be favorable enough to encourage systematic exploratory work to enable us to know its real magnitude. Some experts have estimated that conditions in certain regions of the country place Mexico among nations rich in this type of resource.

GEOTHERMAL RESOURCES

Mexico's tectonic and volcanic characteristics place it among the countries best endowed with geothermal potential. There is a 150 megawatt plant in operation, and it is considered possible that by the end of this century Mexico could have some two thousand megawatts of generating capacity at its disposal in plants using underground steam, with the existing geothermal technology.

NEW TECHNOLOGIES

Renewable energy resources are potentially quite important for Mexico since there are large expanses of arid land with very high sunshine levels.

Various institutions are working on development of solar energy utilization by using photovoltaic systems as well as thermodynamic techniques. Some institutions are working on the development of energy systems based on wind and biomass conversion.

Demand

The demand for energy is equal to that of a developing country, with quite significant growth rates. In areas of the country that could be considered industrialized, such as Mexico City, Monterrey, Guadalajara, and Puebla, energy requirements per capita are relatively high due to industry. Nevertheless, in the rural areas, which contain the largest part of the population and cover the largest part of the territory, consumption is extremely low because of poor economic conditions.

In fact, the high growth rates in energy consumption predicted for the coming decades are congruent with the country's development plans, which attempt to incorporate all of these areas into the economic system.

In the development plans, growth rates in energy demand on the order of 10 percent annually have been assumed for the next twenty

Fig. 3. Formation of the marine shelf of Campeche

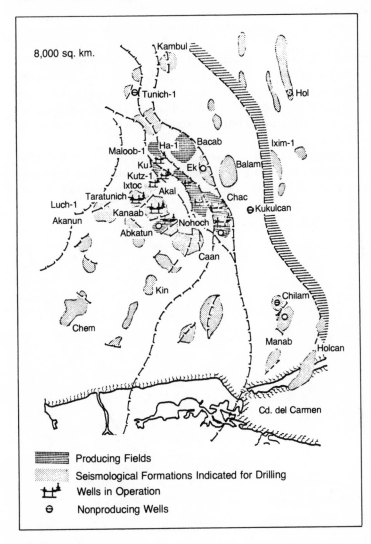

years. Although these goals might be overoptimistic, present day planning makes it necessary to envision such growth levels in order to make
sure that energy resources will be available to achieve the broadest
national development objectives. Part of the energy resources are es-

sential for export, so the country may have the financial resources needed for investment.

Future energy consumption estimates have been relatively conservative with respect to improvements in the efficiency of energy use. This is primarily due to the fact that in developing countries with relatively low levels of consumption, it is more important to have the energy available than to use it efficiently. This by no means implies that there is no awareness of the need to improve efficiency and of the opportunities that conservation and better utilization provide for making the energy resources last longer.

With the Industrial Development Plan that has been launched, electrical consumption ought to grow faster than overall energy consumption, since electricity is a basic input for industry where growth is con-

Fig. 4. Production of crude, condensate, and gas liquids

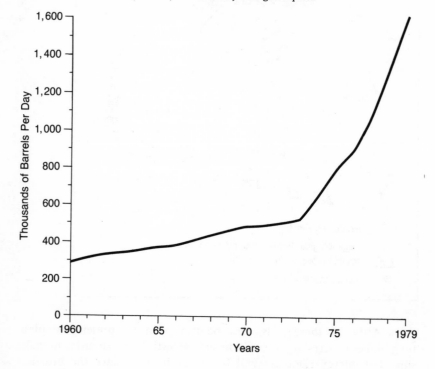

sidered fundamental to the solution of the socioeconomic problems now confronting the country.

During 1980, energy consumption per inhabitant was about 9 million kilocalories. In some of the scenarios considered, the year 2000 would be reached with a total population of about 130 million inhabitants and a per capita energy consumption of about 26 million kilocalories per year. Energy consumption during this twenty-year period would grow at an average annual rate of 8.7 percent. According to this scenario, at the end of the present century Mexico would reach per capita energy consumption levels similar to those presently prevailing in countries like Japan, Italy, or France.

In the case of electrical energy, during the period from 1984 to 2000, an annual average growth rate of 11.4 percent is expected, which would raise the present per capita electricity consumption level from 930 kWh to 4,300 kWh in the year 2000.

Expansion Plans

In order to meet these demands, the energy sector must plan new installations in accordance with energy policy and based on the results of exploration activities. Taking into account the construction periods of these installations, the programs should be made some ten years in advance and should be sufficiently flexible to allow for the modifications required by changes in demand, technology, and time delays.

HYDROCARBONS

Given the reserve situation for this kind of resource, and taking into account the fact that besides the installations needed to produce oil and gas, transformation plants and petrochemical plants must be considered, plans for this sector include not only the energy sector itself but also the petrochemical industry in general. Petroleos Mexicanos is directly responsible for the exploration for, the production of, and the transformation of hydrocarbons, including the primary petrochemical industry. The secondary petrochemical industry, whose potential is considered to be quite important for future years, is being developed by the joint participation of the public and private sectors, including foreign investments.

Fig. 5. Location of refineries and primary distilling capacity

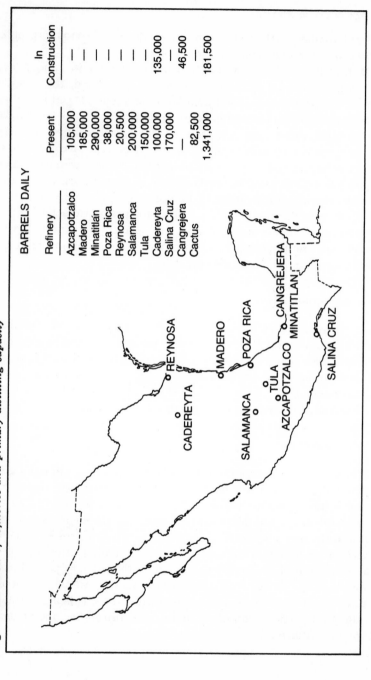

BARRELS DAILY

Refinery	Present	In Construction
Azcapotzalco	105,000	—
Madero	185,000	—
Minatitlán	290,000	—
Poza Rica	38,000	—
Reynosa	20,500	—
Salamanca	200,000	—
Tula	150,000	—
Cadereyta	100,000	135,000
Salina Cruz	170,000	46,500
Cangrejera	—	—
Cactus	82,500	—
	1,341,000	181,500

First priority in the program for expanding the petrochemical industry is the national market. At this writing an export volume of some 1.4 million barrels per day is being contemplated, and since this volume has been set by taking into account the national economy's ability to absorb foreign exchange, it is appropriate to predict that Mexico's share of the international market for oil and gas will not exceed these orders of magnitude in the next few years.

The present level of investment in the petroleum sector of the economy comes to $5 billion per year with growth rates that have been higher than 20 percent in recent years. During the next decade an average growth rate fluctuating between 12 and 16 percent is estimated for the petroleum sector, including the petrochemical industry. As a result, the order of magnitude of investments will be maintained for at least some ten years. Because of the foregoing, even if Mexico does not export oil and gas at volumes much higher than those now being registered, the petroleum sector will show important growth, perhaps the greatest in the national economy.

ELECTRICITY

Historically the growth rate for the electrical sector has been about 10 percent, and it has been predicted that in the coming decades it should increase even more rapidly, for reasons already explained, so that expansion plans that include the installation of additional generating capacity and the transmission and distribution systems this service requires will continue to be among the most important in the country.

Electricity production presents the best opportunity for diversifying primary energy inputs. Even though hydrocarbons will continue to dominate the scene, expansion programs contemplate the installation of hydroelectric, coal-based, and geothermal plants, and the possibility of carrying out a nuclear power program is under study. Its goal is to maintain the relative share of hydrocarbons in the generation of electricity at the present levels.

The amount of investments required for expanding electrical systems is about half that needed for the oil sector—that is, between $2 and $3 billion per year. Since it is convenient to install central power plants which are different from and require higher investments than those using hydrocarbons, it is foreseeable that the investment needs

Fig. 6. National natural gas distribution network

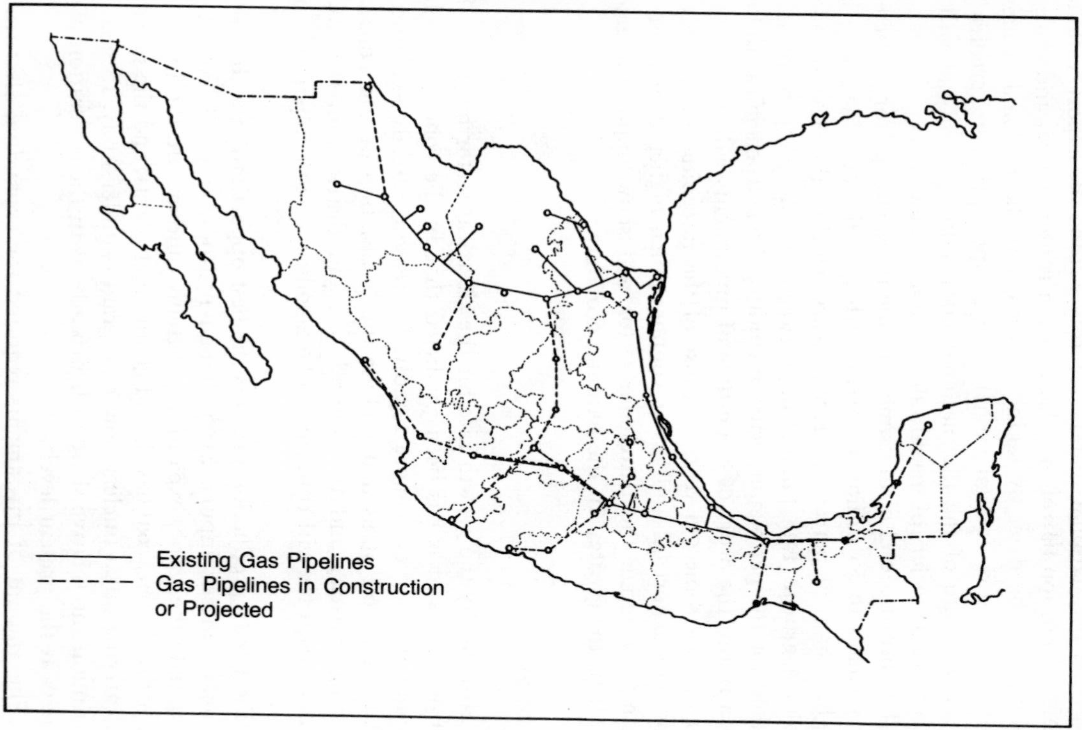

Existing Gas Pipelines
Gas Pipelines in Construction
or Projected

for this sector will grow more in relative terms than will those of the petroleum sector in the next decades.

NONCONVENTIONAL ENERGIES

In the case of renewable energy sources, the focus now being given is to allocate resources for research and development, since under present economic conditions these sources cannot really be considered an alternative to the traditional ones. In fact, nowadays it is considered that the only alternative of any possible importance in the diversification program would be nuclear energy which, to the extent necessary, could take the place of hydrocarbons in producing steam for industry, in addition to playing a role in the electrical sector itself.

Some Policy Considerations

The most important challenge facing a country in a developmental stage similar to Mexico's—i.e., a country which can rely on important hydrocarbon reserves—is that of using them in such a way as to really contribute to a balanced development. The decision to enter the international market in a serious way has been made. During the early 1980s, Mexico will be able to rely on a production structure that will allot half of the oil to the domestic market and the other half to the export market.

The hydrocarbons for the domestic market are essentially oriented toward satisfying a growing demand for energy arising from the growth of all sectors which would eventually be able to act as supports for the infrastructure needed to replace hydrocarbons—both as a main energy source and an export resource. The use to which export-derived funds are put is analogous, that is to say, it is a matter of obtaining financial resources that can guarantee national self-determination, support development, and, eventually, make it possible for hydrocarbons to be replaced by other sources of energy.

The policy has been to convert the surplus hydrocarbons extracted (over and above the amount needed to cover domestic needs) into permanent national sources of wealth which will provide future generations with a well-being which might otherwise have been obtained in the future by further exploiting the nonrenewable resources now being exploited by the present generation.

Fig. 7. Electric network and available power—Federal Electricity Commission, 1978

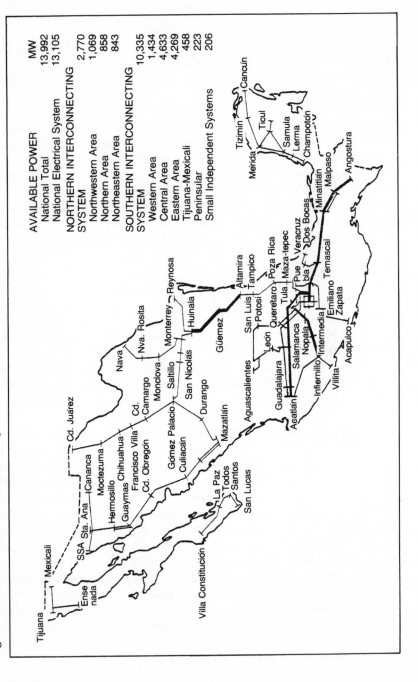

AVAILABLE POWER	MW
National Total	13,992
National Electrical System	13,105
NORTHERN INTERCONNECTING SYSTEM	2,770
Northwestern Area	1,069
Northern Area	858
Northeastern Area	843
SOUTHERN INTERCONNECTING SYSTEM	10,335
Western Area	1,434
Central Area	4,633
Eastern Area	4,269
Tijuana-Mexicali	458
Peninsular	223
Small Independent Systems	206

This is a real challenge since the availability of nonrenewable resources makes it possible to allot greater quantities for export to take the place of the production or services of other sectors that might not be achieved because of internal problems. In fact, the "petrolization" of the country may be defined as the growth, in relative terms, of the petroleum sector in relation to other productive sectors of the economy. The responsibility that has been taken is precisely that of keeping export levels at the minimum necessary to satisfy high priority financial needs in an effort to keep oil development from replacing the development of other sectors of the economy.

On the domestic scene, a decision was made to use energy wealth to promote the country's most efficient development, establishing four industrial ports (in the context of the National Industrial Development Plan) in which industries will receive fiscal incentives and also subsidized prices for the energy they require. In this way it is hoped that growth will be decentralized and a productive infrastructure created that will be agile and competitive on an international scale. By these measures an attempt will be made to succeed in creating wealth that will multiply significantly the value of the hydrocarbons extracted for export.

In the industrialization plan's consideration of external markets, the size of plants to be installed in high-priority industrial development zones will be on the scale necessary to make the processes competitive internationally.

Since one of the characteristics of the oil industry itself is that it is a great income concentrator, it has been decided that a large part of this income shall be transferred into the national economic systems through the tax route. Various measures are now being contemplated, but the most important one is a high tax on exports and a relatively elevated tax on domestic sales. Through the entrance of these resources into the general economic system by the fiscal route, it is possible to bring about a real distribution among high priority sectors of the economy and avoid paternalistic systems.

In addition to internal measures, an attempt has been made to make agreements with countries interested in buying Mexican oil in order to obtain coinvestments and technological contributions to support national development. These agreements envision a commitment to export under usual commercial conditions in exchange for a com-

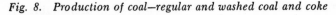

Fig. 8.   Production of coal—regular and washed coal and coke

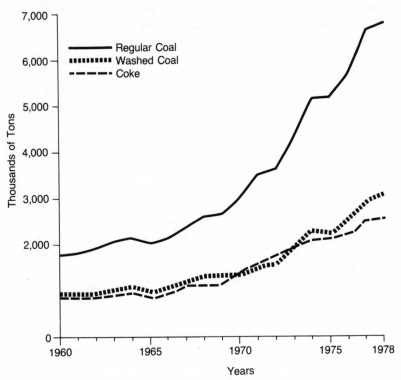

mitment to provide, under favorable terms, the technology and capital to support industry.

It is also fitting to mention here the Mexican President's proposal to the United Nations to the effect that, since energy is so important on a world-wide scale, the U.N. should be concerned about it and formulate a world energy plan which, with due respect for national sovereignty, may resolve the energy problems of all the countries of the world.

Since Mexico also has other energy resources besides hydrocarbons, it has an opportunity to set up an infrastructure to allow it to meet the energy needs of the future, when the most plentiful resource shall have been exhausted. An important policy feature is to seek diversification through exploratory and research efforts, thus making it pos-

Fig. 9. Proven reserves of uranium in tons of U_3O_8

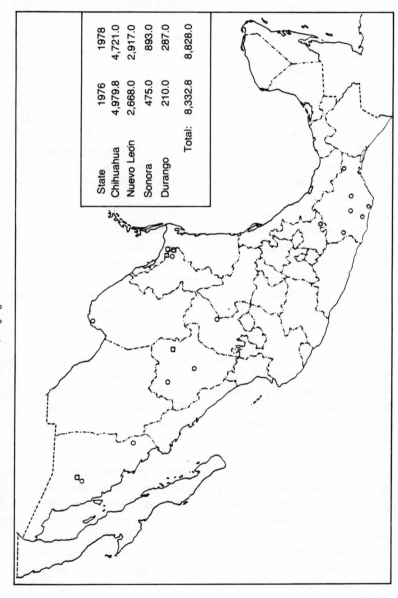

State	1976	1978
Chihuahua	4,979.8	4,721.0
Nuevo León	2,668.0	2,917.0
Sonora	475.0	893.0
Durango	210.0	287.0
Total:	8,332.8	8,828.0

sible to know what resources are available inside the national territory as well as to develop new technologies.

Even though resources for this type of development are limited by the characteristics of the national economy itself, efforts are being made to develop the utilization of renewable resources, among which solar energy is outstanding because of its potential interest. In this case, it is important to keep in mind that the excessive optimism discernible in many countries can lead to serious errors and, eventually, to a scarcity of energy resources to satisfy world needs. Current methods of using solar energy prove to be antieconomical, except in those cases where the cost of supplying energy does not matter, as, for example, remote educational systems based on television, rural communications, and signaling.

The fantasy existing in many circles with respect to the contribution solar energy could make (using present techniques) could be dangerous, since its incorporation might be planned on a scale that might be well above what could actually be accomplished. In line with these ideas, it seems that in Mexico it would be prudent to allocate significant efforts to research and development, but the use of solar energy should not be incorporated into energy development programs until sufficient technological development has occurred to make its use practical.

Since the energy sector is highly capital-intensive, the domestic manufacture of capital goods for that sector should be encouraged. In that regard, important steps have already been taken toward the manufacture of equipment associated with the public service electrical industry. For practical reasons, it is a case of making these developments through coinvestments with external technology suppliers, on the condition that Mexican capital plays a majority role.

Internal energy prices have traditionally been much lower than prices in other countries; this, in the past, was in obedience to the policy of fomenting national development. Nevertheless, there is an awareness that these implicit subsidies lead to a squandering of resources, so it has been decided that they should be raised gradually to bring them up to a level more commensurate with levels prevailing in the rest of the world. In this way an attempt is being made to rationalize energy use, since it has been widely demonstrated that if prices are unfair it is practically impossible to optimize energy consumption systems to guarantee rational use.

Laura R. Randall

3

Mexican Development and Its Effects upon United States Trade

Developing Nations and the Changing Structure of Trade

Mexican development and its effects upon United States trade highlight a new phenomenon pointed out by W. Arthur Lewis: developing nations are growing more rapidly than the highly industrialized world. The growth of developing nations can provide the extra demand needed to pull their richer trading partners out of a recession and provide them with opportunities for the utilization of their otherwise unemployed goods, services, labor, capital, technology, and entrepreneurship. This is true of the relationship between Mexico and the United States, despite the fact that the United States accounts for a larger share of Mexico's trade than Mexico does for that of the United States. In the first quarter of 1980 the U.S. took 73.8 percent of Mexico's exports, and 68.4 percent of Mexican imports came from the U.S. By mid-1980, Mexico was our third most important trading partner. In January–September 1980, Mexico bought 6.5 percent of U.S. exports

LAURA R. RANDALL *is a professor of economics at Hunter College of the City University of New York. She has published extensively in the areas of Latin American economic history and development. Her most recent book is* An Economic History of Argentina in the Twentieth Century. *Dr. Randall has written several recent articles on Mexican and Latin American oil policy and its impact on Latin American domestic and international policy making.*

and supplied 5.2 percent of U.S. imports. In 1979 it absorbed 3.6 percent of U.S. direct foreign investment abroad, and, in recent years, it has imported more professional workers than it has sent abroad.

As developing nations grow richer and more complex in their economic structure, their trade becomes more varied. Mexico's ability to supply oil and natural gas dominates the popular press. The underlying shift in Mexican trade patterns, in contrast, reflects the increasing sophistication of the Mexican economy. Manufactures have increased, as a share of nonoil merchandise exports, from 17 percent in 1965 to 50 percent of Mexican exports in January–March 1980. Within the manufacturing sector, the overall pattern from 1965 to 1979 was the striking growth of machinery and transport equipment exports, which provided 14 percent of nonoil merchandise exports in 1979. Chemicals, food products and beverages, and clothing and footwear continued to be major exports. Iron and steel exports fell sharply, in part due to Mexico's rapid economic growth, which also reduced exports of machinery and transport equipment in early 1980.

As developing nations grow stronger, they are able to influence the international organizations to which they belong and are eventually able to modify their structure. International trade is increasingly carried out under rules that reflect developing nations' preferences. Thus, the Latin American Free Trade Association was replaced at the end of 1980 by the Latin American Integration Association, which favored bilateral and multilateral accords. Latin American nations were not initially able to influence the General Agreement on Trade and Tariffs (GATT) as much as they had wished; many of them have refused to adhere to GATT. In 1980 Mexico decided to postpone joining GATT, in part to protect its small- and medium-scale industry, and in part because GATT disapproves of bilateral arrangements which are thought to be a step backward from multilateralism.

In Latin America, however, bilateral agreements are the easiest to form and, in fact, are necessary precursors of broader economic integration. In Mexico, bilateral agreements are used to obtain scarce technology, especially in the energy sector, that possibly could not be obtained by any other trading technique. Mexico's preference for bilateral trade packages, such as those signed with Japan, Spain, Switzerland, Canada, and Brazil, in contrast to foreign trade without links, was reaffirmed by President Lopez Portillo in his fourth report to the nation on September 1, 1980. United States–Mexican trade in the

1980s, therefore, is likely to be placed increasingly on a bilateral basis in which the items to be exchanged are specified.

Mexico is the most important of the developing nations with which we trade. Its economic growth will strongly influence the U.S. economy through the level and composition of trade, through compensating movements of factors of production, and through changes in the rules of the game under which trade is carried out. An assessment of each of these influences on the United States can best be made by examining Mexico's development policy and the ways in which the anticipated economic development will affect U.S. trade.

Mexican Development Policy

DEVELOPMENT POLICY BEFORE 1976

Since independence, Mexican governments have had a strong and continuing interest in fostering the economic development and economic self-reliance of the nation. Shifts in policy and tactics reflect changing perceptions of how to achieve these goals. In the nineteenth century, the national government created the infrastructure necessary for development. The outlying regions of the nation were brought under government control; the government actively sought foreign investment. It promoted railroad building and increased the number of schools. It imported technology by seeking immigrants, who brought their skills with them. It also changed the structure of land-holding by expropriating both the church and indigenous community landholders. Although expropriating the church and *campesinos* had very different political motives and effects, both moves brought land and its products into the market.

In the twentieth century, government creation and support of economic activity has continued. The establishment and growth of *Nacional Financiera* provided much of the basis for development financing; extended transportation and education have helped the population take advantage of market opportunities. The government has attempted to increase its control over the economy by changing the structure of domestic markets by land reform, nationalizing some industries, and Mexicanizing others.

Within a broad policy of government responsibility for national welfare, there have been cycles of emphasizing first economic and then social solutions to national problems. The theories used to justify government actions, and the strategies also used to achieve national aims, have shifted with each administration. This has meant that until the Presidency of Jose Lopez Portillo, plans were rarely considered for more than the six-year term of office.

Mexican economic policy has been criticized on the grounds that it has emphasized the growth of large industry and agriculture, for example, by setting high minimum sizes for bidding on government contracts and by emphasizing research and development for crops produced for export by capital-intensive methods, rather than for crops produced for Mexican consumption in a labor-intensive manner which form the basis of traditional agriculture.

These criticisms reflect key questions for Mexican development policy: how to improve the productive capacity of small and medium-sized ventures, and how to decrease monopolies in local markets without alienating Mexico's most powerful producers. The hostile relations between business and government in 1976 worsened the economic recession and the effects of the two devaluations of the peso. The need to repair these relations determined the form of Mexican economic policy promulgated by President Lopez Portillo.

DEVELOPMENT POLICY UNDER PRESIDENT JOSE LOPEZ PORTILLO

When President Lopez Portillo took office in 1976, Mexico was a country with serious economic problems and considerable internal dissension. Rapid population growth, massive foreign debt, net oil and food imports, continuing but inconclusive invasions of land by peasants, and two devaluations had led to a decline in the private sector's confidence in the government. Rumors of political assassinations of businessmen and a possible coup against the government abounded. Mexican labor and capital poured into the United States. The government was faced with the choice of either creating business confidence and simultaneously attracting both Mexican funds which had been sent abroad as well as new foreign investment, or of closing the economy to foreign influence by limiting the flow of capital abroad, increasing favoritism for Mexican over foreign suppliers, and, where necessary, either increasing credit to private business to keep it afloat or taking over business to maintain employment. The former course was chosen.

As a result, the short-run objectives of the government were to create confidence, contain inflation, and plan for structural modification of the economy. In the medium term, the government hoped to increase the complexity of economic structure, to shift the location of economic development (by building up less developed areas within Mexico and by limiting the growth of the metropolitan area), and to reduce unemployment. Long-term development goals have been announced and are in part binding, as it would be wasteful to abandon the construction of plant and equipment before its completion unless the project in question was remarkably high cost and inefficient.

The program to restore confidence in the Mexican government encompassed political, administrative, and economic reforms designed to broaden participation both in the electoral process and in economic decision making. The broad economic plans of the government are contained in the National Industrial Development Plan and in the Global Development Plan for 1980–1982, as well as in presidential addresses and related documents. The ways in which these plans are to be implemented are spelled out in Alliance for Production agreements between industry and government and in the reports of government enterprises, such as PEMEX, the national oil firm, and the CFE, which supplies Mexico's electric power.

The National Industrial Development Plan—The National Industrial Development Plan was announced in March 1979. It states that Mexico's oil revenues will be used to finance the nation's economic development. Although many officials urged that the development plan should emphasize immediate increases in employment, even if this meant a low or moderate rate of economic growth, the government selected a plan which emphasizes a high rate of economic growth and provides for slower increases in employment, with full employment being achieved in 1990.

In order to improve the standard of living, the government stated that it would

> strengthen the production of basic consumer goods, give an impulse to high-productivity areas oriented toward the export market, take full and integrated advantage of the country's natural resources, foster the growth of the capital goods industry, achieve territorial decentralization of economic activities by orienting investment mainly toward the coasts and borders, and . . . articulate small and medium-sized companies with the large firms and thus attenuate the trend to oligopolies.

The plan takes the agricultural growth rate as given and estimates that it will be one-third of the average growth rate between 1975 and 1990. Measures designed to improve the agroindustrial sector and decrease the nation's projected reliance on food imports were announced in 1980. (These measures are discussed later in this chapter.)

Mining, trade, and services are expected to decrease their share in national product during these years. Especially high growth rates are planned for oil and petrochemicals, construction, electricity, and manufactures. The development of these sectors is particularly important for United States–Mexican trade relations, both because a large share of the capital goods needed for economic expansion will be imported and because oil, petrochemicals, and manufactures increasingly will be exported to the United States. The projected economic structure of Mexico is shown in Table 1.

TABLE 1.   SECTORIAL SHARE OF GROSS DOMESTIC PRODUCT AND PAID
           ECONOMICALLY ACTIVE POPULATION—1975, 1982, 1990

	Product			Employment			Share of Product Per Worker Compared to National Average		
	1975	1982	1990	1975	1982	1990	1975	1982	1990
Total	100	100	100	100	100	100	100	100	100
Primary	9.3	6.8	3.9	35.0	29.2	19.0	26.6	23.2	20.5
Industrial	35.6	41.4	44.4	27.6	28.6	28.1	129.0	144.8	158.0
Trade & Services	55.1	51.8	51.7	37.4	42.2	52.9	147.3	122.7	97.7

Source: Comercio Exterior de México, June 1979.

The projected figures are startling because they indicate an increasing gap in productivity per worker in agriculture compared to the rest of the nation. This was especially hard to accept because of the large and increasing share of food in Mexico's import bill: agricultural goods accounted for 10 percent of merchandise imports in January–March 1980 and are expected to rise to 38.1 billion pesos ($1.7 billion) in 1975 prices by 1990, absorbing 54 percent of the income Mexico expects to receive from oil exports. Thus, both strategic considerations and balance of payment concerns led the government to prepare a special agroindustrial plan.

The National Industrial Development Plan is therefore part, but not all, of the blueprint for the growth of the Mexican economy. If the targets set are achieved, it will affect United States–Mexican trade relations in several ways.

It will increase both income and income per capita. Mexican–U.S. trade increases more rapidly than does the income growth in either nation. Mexico's richest citizens can be expected to increase their purchases of housing, furnishings, medical care, education, recreation and culture, communications, insurance, and gifts. U.S. sales of services to Mexico's upper classes probably will increase more strongly than will their sales of basic consumer goods. Mexico's upper-middle-income groups have similar consumption patterns; they are likely to increase their expenditures on cars, although these are largely made in Mexico. The poorer half of Mexico's population is more likely to increase its expenditures on clothing and cars, but is less likely to purchase imported goods than their richer compatriots.

The United States has a comparative advantage in services, which economists describe as "capital-intensive industries." Specialized education, research and development, and medical care are costly to provide and are usually developed in a market which has abundant supplies of capital and a large number of people who use these services. The large and increasing number of Mexicans who come to the United States to purchase such services indicates that as Mexican industrialization increases, the export of services by the United States to Mexico will grow concurrently.

Mexico has decided to grow rapidly, at least through 1990. If growth were to take place at a more moderate pace, then the Mexican capital goods industry might well be able to increase its ability to expand its production of those capital goods which are already made in Mexico. It might also be able to increase the number of capital goods which it produces.

Rapid industrialization, however, requires the immediate availability of capital goods. As a result, many of them will have to be imported. The World Bank, in a highly critical report, states that in the mid-1970s, "the preferential access of government agencies to imports has drastically reduced the domestic market for capital equipment, much of which Mexico could probably produce fairly efficiently itself."

To the extent that this situation still prevails, the Mexican government's plans to carry out industrialization by using government agencies implies a substantial increase in imports of capital goods by these agencies. As the United States supplies more than two-thirds of Mexico's imports, most of the goods are likely to be purchased in the United States. The National Industrial Development Plan estimates that in 1990 Mexico will import $8.6 billion of electrical machinery (in 1975 prices), $7.6 billion of metal-machine products, $1.7 billion of basic chemicals, $1.7 billion of transport equipment, and $1.6 billion of metallic ores.

Overall investment and import plans for key agencies in the National Industrial Development Plan are as follows. Total physical investment planned for PEMEX for 1979–1986 is equal to $23.2 billion (in 1977 prices). Some 48 percent of the investment ($11 billion) requires the acquisition of goods not currently made in Mexico. Mexico has the ability to supply a large share of capital goods needed in exploration and drilling activities; it is less able to supply them for refineries and imports 80 percent of materials and equipment for the petrochemical sector. PEMEX purchases will account for about 5 percent of gross industrial production from 1977 to 1986 and will have the greatest impact on Mexico's nonelectrical machinery industry, purchasing 24 percent of its output. Critics concede that it takes years to bring into production plants which make the goods made by PEMEX and that, in consequence, "a good part of the benefits deriving from developments in the oil industry in Mexico will continue to be transferred abroad." In 1978 PEMEX accounted for 3.8 percent of Mexico's imports.

The picture in the electric power industry is different: 88 percent of the traditional equipment needed for anticipated investment for 1979 to 1986 is available in Mexico; almost half of the imports will probably originate in the United States. Originally, the electric sector planned to import $2.5 billion worth of equipment (in 1978 prices); this number will be increased as Mexico has repeatedly increased its planned expansion of the electric power industry beyond the targets set in the National Industrial Development Plan. The picture is less clear for the probable suppliers of equipment to the nuclear-electric power industry. Delays in filling private contracts and U.S. government suspension of delivery of nuclear fuel in 1978–79 cast serious doubt on the reliability of the United States as a supplier of goods for this sector.

The size of capital goods imports for the fertilizer industry will be about $307 million—some 16 percent of the capital goods supplies. Imports for coal mines will be at least $135 million by 1982; payments for engineering licensing and technology will be $700 million between 1979 and 1982. From 1979 to 1986, the minimum estimate of imports by parastate organizations is $14.1 billion. Even though Mexican capital goods capacity will expand, parastate imports will be significant at least through 1990. Total investment by parastate organizations between 1979 and 1990 is projected at $153 billion (in 1978 prices).

Private sector expansion and demand for capital goods imports are harder to estimate, both because of current and anticipated under-utilization of capacity and because of increasing competition from imports. The National Industrial Development Plan estimates that the economy will grow between 8 and 10 percent annually and that the capital goods industry will grow at a rate of 18 to 20 percent. This is not sufficient to provide the investment goods needed for Mexico's projected economic growth.

In the mid-1970s, Mexico imported one-fifth of its machinery and equipment. Within this group almost 50 percent of industrial machinery was imported, about 20 percent of electrical machinery and transport equipment, and about 6 percent of metal products. The share of imported capital goods to total demand is much higher in Mexico than in Argentina and Brazil, which are at similar stages of economic development, and has serious implications for Mexico's balance of payments position: in 1979, 39 percent of merchandise imports was investment goods. This large share of the import bill reflects three factors: large government imports to carry out its development plan, increased income generated by the oil boom, and the removal of licensing and other restrictions on imports. The rate at which imports increased in relation to the increase in income almost quadrupled in 1979, in contrast to the level which had obtained for the previous twenty years.

It is important to note, however, that the National Industrial Development Plan and the imports of equipment by the government which it stimulated are not the major cause of Mexico's $3.4 billion deficit on trade in goods. The government accounted for 32 percent of goods imports, the private sector for 68 percent; private sector imports increased 2.4 times as fast as those of the government in 1979. The determinants of Mexican–U.S. international trade are not the focus of the National Industrial Development Plan; they are, however, discussed in the *Plan Global de Desarrollo,* which is described later.

The National Industrial Development Plan includes the use of subsidies to encourage the growth of key sectors. Where the planned expansion more than meets national needs, Mexico hopes to export the "surplus" goods. This may be more difficult to do under GATT rules, which provide that nations may levy countervailing duties in the case of export subsidies. When goods are exported at prices below those on the domestic market, they are "dumped," and antidumping duties can be imposed by the United States. Yet even if the goods exported to the United States are sold at the same price as that obtaining on the domestic market, if this price is less than the estimated cost of production, duties may be imposed. U.S. law states that in the case of countries which do not adhere to GATT, countervailing duties can be levied on dutiable articles without an investigation and determination of material injury. In the case of an article which is free of duty, material injury to a United States industry must be proved for a countervailing duty to be imposed.

Mexico uses subsidies to stimulate production. In September 1980, President Lopez Portillo argued that many subsidies no longer meet their initial objectives and benefit middle-income and rich Mexicans, who do not need subsidies, as well as poor Mexicans who do. During the 1970s, he estimated that $13.3 billion of subsidies—some 72 percent of the total—was not spent on socially necessary ends or investment and should be decisively, but not brusquely, eliminated. Subsidies on goods for popular consumption will remain in place, as will those initiated under the National Industrial Development Plan. These include reduced rates on electricity, natural gas, fuel oil, and basic petrochemicals granted to firms which invest in designated regions. The reduced rates will be below those prevailing on the domestic market; the latter will be kept below international levels as part of government incentives to invest.

In addition, in order to stimulate the export of manufactures, firms which export these goods could apply for subsidies of up to 100 percent of the import duties levied on machines and equipment they import and use in production.

The first of the two policies mentioned seems likely to cause difficulty if Mexico wishes to export to the United States: subsidized raw materials are used to produce petrochemicals; they seem especially likely to be subject to countervailing duties. Exports of secondary petrochemicals are expected to grow 19 percent annually, reaching 1.391 billion pesos in 1975 prices ($111 million, at the 1975 exchange rate of 12.5 pesos to the dollar) by 1990; related fertilizer exports are expected to grow almost 10 percent a year, reaching 773 million pesos ($61.84 million). Oil and basic petrochemicals also will grow 19 percent yearly, reaching an estimated 69.464 billion pesos ($5.6 billion), a sum which may have to be revised upward to reflect both Mexico's larger than expected crude oil output and higher than expected world oil prices.

Mexico does not wish to import products derived from petroleum. Efficient refineries apparently require a scale of operation that yields an output larger than the Mexican market is thought likely to absorb by 1990. Yet even if expanded agricultural activity requires the use of much of the fertilizer which planners had initially thought would be exported, the problem of ensuring petrochemical exports remains. Since competition from the United States and other petrochemical producers is likely to be severe, Mexico will probably seek to ensure these exports by choosing among the following alternatives: (a) including petrochemicals in a tied bilateral trade package with the United States, (b) seeking increased trade with nations less likely to impose countervailing duties, (c) seeking the minority participation in the secondary petrochemical industry of U.S.–based multinational corporations or their affiliates with the expectation that they will seek favorable treatment for these products since importing them will increase their profits.

The 1973 law to promote Mexican investment and to regulate foreign investment limits foreign investment in secondary petrochemicals to 40 percent and excludes foreign investment from petroleum, other hydrocarbons, and basic petrochemicals. A rough index of the possible opportunity for foreign investment, or of the need for foreign funds, is that planned gross fixed investment in private secondary petrochemicals is 21 billion pesos in 1975 prices; 40 percent of this sum is

$672 million. If foreign participation in exchange for guaranteed exports is arranged, Mexico will have found a way to repay foreign investment without the balance of payments and exchange rate problems that result from the use of foreign investment to produce goods which are sold only on the domestic market. (In the latter case, it is difficult to provide the foreign exchange needed for payment of profits or repatriation of capital.)

Looking beyond the petrochemical industry, the National Industrial Development Plan estimates that 5 percent of Mexico's investment funds will come from foreign sources in 1990. An indication of U.S. firms' investment is given in Table 2. Some $25 billion (in 1978 prices)

TABLE 2.   CAPITAL EXPENDITURES IN MEXICO BY MAJORITY-OWNED
FOREIGN AFFILIATES OF U.S. COMPANIES, 1978–1980 *

	(in millions of dollars)		
Category	1978	1979	1980
All industries	347	678	1,003
Mining & smelting	4	6	9
Petroleum	1	1	17
Manufacturing			
Total	276	560	859
Food products	52	80	110
Paper & allied products	27	36	39
Chemical & allied products	59	82	90
Rubber products	8	11	26
Primary & fabricated metals	22	42	**
Machinery, except electrical	60	75	123
Electrical machinery	8	10	19
Transportation equipment	31	203	**
Other manufacturing	9	20	44
Trade	41	78	77
Other industries	24	34	41

* Based on a survey taken in December 1979
** Suppressed to avoid disclosure of individual reporters
Source: Survey of Current Business, March 1980.

of goods, not including petroleum or income from services performed in border assembly plants, will be exported; goods imported will amount to $90 billion. Oil exports are estimated at $12.5 billion, and earnings from work done at border plants will total $14 billion. It is striking that Mexico anticipates an export of services of $46 billion, compared to goods exports of $38 billion.

Imports of goods and services are to be $103 billion, leaving Mexico with an $18 billion deficit on goods and services if the relationship between the prices of imports and of exports does not change. Payment by the public sector of interest on the foreign debt will reach an estimated $8.5 billion. The prices which Mexico received for its exports compared with those paid for imports improved 71 percent between 1977 and the spring of 1980. Although Mexico underestimated its probable receipts from sales of oil, it seriously underestimated its imports in 1979 and 1980. The government believes that the surge in imports is a temporary phenomenon and that early 1980 figures may indicate a favorable balance of trade with the United States. The figures nonetheless reinforce the conclusion that Mexico will need to obtain foreign exchange either from foreign borrowing, foreign investment, or increased sales of petroleum.

Revised estimates of Mexican oil export receipts should reflect the fact that Mexico is now able to obtain better terms for its oil in world oil markets than it did from 1975 to 1976. Projections using 1975 oil price indicators are misleading, while the shift in technical characteristics of the oil sold by Mexico also made projections inaccurate. On the other hand, it is harder to bring in offshore than onshore oil, and Mexico's large demand for oil for domestic use left a smaller share for exports, requiring a slight increase in production to meet export targets.

The changing conditions surrounding petroleum sales underscore the difficulty of projecting economic conditions and outcomes for long periods of time. The National Industrial Development Plan gives prominent place to the plans for key sectors. In contrast, the *Plan Global de Desarrollo, 1980–82*, provides a general statement of Mexican development goals and of plans utilized to reach them. It also analyzes the conditions which determine the behavior of key economic variables.

The two plans were prepared at different times by different ministries, so that each document has its partisans. The alternate vision of the Global Development Plan, in this case with respect to balance of payments, is analyzed in the next section, in part because this plan was frequently mentioned by President Lopez Portillo in September 1980, in contrast to the infrequent mention of the earlier National Industrial Development Plan.

The Global Development Plan—According to the Global Development Plan, exports depend upon conditions in the United States, and imports depend upon the Mexican economy and the availability of foreign financing. The export of manufactures depends on world economic activity which is represented by real U.S. income, the relationship between wholesale prices for Mexican and U.S. nonagricultural goods, and the exchange rate. There is no evidence that the degree of capacity utilization in Mexico affects exports.

The change in U.S. income is associated more closely with Mexican goods exports, services performed by border assembly plants, and earnings from tourism than are other variables. On the other hand, income from frontier transactions varies more strongly with the exchange rate, lagged one year, than with U.S. income.

Mexican consumer goods imports most closely reflect Mexican private consumer demand and U.S. consumer prices adjusted for the exchange rate. Mexican agricultural production has a weak but significant relation to consumer goods imports. Imports of capital goods are strongly associated with real total investment and less strongly with the exchange rate and with appropriate prices in Mexico and the United States. The importation of intermediate goods varies most closely with external financing (public sector debt and net private capital inflow) and the exchange rate. Mexican tourist expenditures and frontier transactions depend upon gross product, adjusted for terms of trade, and on relative prices, adjusted for the exchange rate.

These relationships are plausible, but do not exclude the possibility that other explanations of Mexican trade would be equally accurate. The policy implications of the relationships outlined in the Global Development Plan are that to increase earnings from exports of manufactured goods, Mexico must either reduce its rate of inflation or devalue its currency in the short run, and in the long run it must increase the productivity of the manufacturing sector.

In 1980 it was often suggested that the peso would be devalued in the near future and that the government would reduce the rate at which it increased the supply of money and credit. At the same time, the government attempted to increase productivity by creating joint commissions of government, labor, and private sector representatives to study productivity by both requiring employers to provide increased training of labor and providing infrastructure.

Since Mexican exports depend upon U.S. income and the economic policies and performance of the United States have been criticized by many varied observers, Mexico reasonably could be expected to try to protect itself from the erratic course of U.S. policy and from fluctuations in the U.S. economy. This can be achieved by signing medium- or long-term bilateral trade agreements with the United States as well as with other nations, by increasing the number of trading partners and number of goods and services traded, and by joining with other nations in commodity agreements designed to even out fluctuations in sales and prices. Mexico has, in fact, made several explicit and implicit moves in these directions.

Mexico's capacity to import indirectly depends upon conditions in the United States. Mexican consumer demand is influenced by the level of national income, which reflects domestic spending and the balance of trade. Since exports depend on U.S. economy, their size influences consumer demand and imports. Mexico has made importing easier by removing quantitative restrictions and by easing administrative procedures; moreover, Mexico is promoting growth at a rate of 8 to 10 percent a year. Both actions will increase consumer demand for imports.

Mexico can reduce part of its demand for consumer goods imports by increasing the domestic supply of agricultural products. The government, as has been its practice since 1976, has attempted to define the actions needed, the persons who should undertake them, and the time and place where they should be carried out. In 1980 it promulgated the establishment of the Mexican Food System, which is to cover all aspects of the food industry by including agriculture and animal raising, fishing, food-processing industries, and food technology. In a statement that has since been modified, the Global Development Plan stated that Mexico would promote self-sufficiency in each of the key subsystems of the national food system and that this, together with an improved distribution system for basic foods, would provide adequate nourishment for all Mexicans.

The growth rate for agriculture was to be 4.1 percent—higher than that assumed in the National Industrial Development Plan. Mexico was to be self-sufficient in corn and beans by 1982, and in other sectors by 1985. Mexico was to achieve these goals by directing 22 percent of public investment to agriculture from 1980 to 1982. In related measures, the government provided improved food prices, credit, packaging, and transport in 1980, and developed a program to increase the production of agricultural tractors. The government also expropriated some large landholdings, stating that part of its reason was to shift land use from animal raising to food production. However, the President stated that land use would not be shifted from export crops to grain; lands devoted to export crops are not well suited to grain production, and such a shift in land use could decrease the availability of food. Mexico, therefore, will probably continue to import grain, especially wheat, for several years.

It did not seem likely that Mexico would try to reduce imports of capital goods in the early 1980s; the partial opening of the economy to increased competition in capital goods and a consequent increase of the technology effectively available to Mexican industry seemed likely to continue. At the same time, the domestic capital goods industry was to be stimulated by the use of subsidies and fiscal incentives, which might enable it to meet the increased competition.

Similarly, Mexico did not so much seek to limit imports of intermediate goods as to improve the conditions which made them possible. Intermediate goods imports were thought to depend upon the availability of financing; in the late 1970s, Mexico improved the terms and structure of the public sector foreign debt and regulated private capital inflow.

Mexican expenditures on tourism and frontier transactions were not the subject of special measures to limit them. A reduction in this category of spending seemed likely only if Mexico controlled the rate of inflation, devalued the peso, or improved the quality and quantity of goods and services available in Mexico. This would make purchases in Mexico more attractive than purchases in the United States. Since the government could not limit many of Mexico's imports without reducing the rate of economic growth, emphasis necessarily was placed on the promotion of exports. In this respect, border assembly plants were of particular importance.

Trade Regimes and Benefits from Trade—Mexico's border assembly plants, called *maquiladoras*, benefit from U.S. tariff items 806.30 and 807.00 which exempt the cost of U.S. components from tariffs; the dutiable value of assembled imports is based on the cost of labor and other inputs supplied by the assembling country, certain "assists" provided by U.S. firms and individuals in that country, and the cost of transport from the United States to the assembly site. Their growth is also the result of Mexico's Border Industrialization Program, which was established in 1965 to provide employment for *braceros* who could no longer legally enter the United States. The program complemented existing free-zone legislation and allowed foreigners to use trust arrangements with Mexican credit institutions for the purpose of acquiring partial control over industrial sites in border regions. This avoided violation of the constitutional provision which bans foreign ownership of land or water along the frontier. In 1977 the *maquiladora* program was expanded by permitting firms set up to supply the domestic market to engage in assembly operations as long as the exported items had at least 20 percent of local value added.

Maquiladora operations affect the Mexican economy through wages, which make up 61 percent of *maquiladora* charges, and through purchases of local raw materials and packing, which account for 7 percent of *maquiladora* charges. The remainder of *maquiladora* expenditures are spread among many activities. Since *maquiladora* operations take advantage of low-cost labor, it is not surprising that goods produced in *maquiladoras* are more labor-intensive than other Mexican exports and that *maquiladoras* employ five women for every man.

The dutiable value of *maquiladora* shipments to the United States has grown from $3 million in 1966 to $536 million in 1976, and $1,027 million in 1979. In 1976 *maquiladora* exports were equal to more than half of Mexican exports to the U.S. of manufactures, excluding chemicals and some food, oil, and fiber products. About 66 percent of *maquiladora* exports consisted of items such as electronic parts, television parts, and communication equipment. Clothing exports under the *maquiladora* program were much less important (see Table 3).

The *maquiladora* program is not considered beneficial by all observers. United States labor has urged the repeal of tariff items 806.30 and 807.00 on the grounds that they export jobs that should be filled in the United States. The United States Tariff Commission ruled that repeal of these items would lead to the substitution of imports without U.S. components rather than with U.S. components, thereby reducing rather than increasing U.S. payrolls.

TABLE 3.   UNITED STATES IMPORTS OF MAQUILADORA PRODUCTS
AND TOTAL IMPORTS FROM MEXICO, 1979 (THOUSANDS OF DOLLARS)

Category	Total Value (1)	Dutiable Value (2)	Total Imports (3)	Col. 1 ÷ Col. 3 %	Col. 2 ÷ Col. 1 %
Food and animals	—	—	1,641,259	—	—
Paper and wood products	52,612	13,382	164,748	31.9	25.4
Yarn, fabric, and clothing	169,944	52,509	245,987	69.1	30.9
Chemicals and petroleum	86	29	3,350,417	—	33.7
Ceramics, glass, and minerals	6,247	5,516	182,678	3.4	88.3
Metal, machines, electric equipment, and transport equipment	1,628,968	855,065	2,551,397	63.9	52.5
Leather, rubber, and other manufactures	207,708	89,338	393,933	52.7	43.0
Returned goods, art, religious articles	—	—	165,772	—	—
Goods valued at less than $251	—	—	117,188		
Total	2,065,564	1,015,839	8,813,378	23.4	49.2

Source: United States Bureau of the Census, IA 236-A (2/2/80); United States Bureau of the Census, IA 236 (AN 1979).

The importance of the *maquiladora* program for Mexico's ability to export is highlighted by the existing alternatives, which include exporting to the United States under the Generalized System of Preferences granted to imports from developing countries, accepting quotas on exports of selected items under special agreements, or exporting under provisions of the United States Tariff Code.

The Generalized System of Preferences, established in 1974, authorizes the President to grant duty-free treatment to more than 2,700 eligible articles imported from designated developing nations for up to ten years, ending January 3, 1985. The nations must follow specified rules of the game regarding international trade and expropriated foreign property and may not be members of OPEC unless they sign trade treaties with the United States and assure the United States fair access to goods at reasonable prices. In 1979 Congress required the suspension of Generalized System of Preferences privileges if a country interrupted or ended the delivery of supplies of petroleum and petroleum products to the United States.

Except in specified circumstances, which include a bilateral trade treaty between a developing nation and the United States, Generalized System of Preferences treatment is suspended if a developing nation's exports of an article to the United States during the year have an appraised value whose ratio to $25 million exceeds the ratio of the U.S. gross national product (GNP) of that year to the GNP of 1974. This sum was $33.5 million in 1978 and $37.3 million in 1979. Generalized System of Preferences treatment is also suspended if the ratio to the appraised value of total U.S. imports of that article equals or exceeds 50 percent. The 1979 Trade Agreements Act waived the latter proviso in cases where the value of the exports divided by $1 million was not greater than the ratio of the GNP in the year the exports took place to the GNP of 1979.

These limits in preferential treatment may make it necessary for Mexico to plan to export moderate amounts of many goods to the United States, rather than large amounts of goods where its comparative advantage is greatest. Indeed, when possible, Mexico exports goods to the United States under tariff items 806.30 and 807.00 instead of under GSP provisions: in 1976, Mexican Generalized System of Preferences to the United States came to only 25 percent of the value of Mexican industry shipments. The advantage is that tariff items 806.30 and 807.00 do not contain the ceiling limits on value exported to the United States that the GSP imposes. In point of fact, many Mexican exports have reached the ceiling limits, which forces the exporter either to stop production or to sell at a higher price which results from being subject to the higher (non–GSP) United States import duty. However, there are disadvantages faced by *maquiladoras* exporting under 806.30 and 807.00: locally made components do not receive duty-free treatment.

The differences among the ways in which goods produced or worked on in Mexico enter the United States raise several questions about who benefits most from Mexican industrialization and Mexican exports to the United States. Goods entering the United States under tariff item 806.30 must be imported by or for the account of the original U.S. exporter; this is not required for imports under tariff item 807.00. It would be interesting to know the degree to which Mexican citizens own firms which are incorporated in the United States, especially those which use the tariff items in question.

The question of Mexican ownership of U.S. firms has been largely ignored; the question of U.S. and other foreign ownership of Mexican firms has been studied and has led to detailed regulation of foreign investment in Mexico. Some observers argue that if foreigners own as much as 25 percent of a firm, they probably control it, especially if host country ownership is dispersed among many shareholders. It is also stated that almost half of the world trade takes place within multinational corporations; this observation applies to Mexico. In the early 1970s, foreign firms' exports of manufactures were almost 25 percent greater than their share of production in Mexican industry. Foreign ownership was concentrated in industries with higher than average rates of growth. Gross figures suggest that foreign firms concentrate in the production of goods made by using capital-intensive methods, while Mexican firms concentrate on the export of goods made by using labor-intensive methods.

In the mid-1970s a dollar of exports by foreign firms created only 56 percent of the employment that would result for a dollar of exports by Mexican firms. This estimate, however, probably should be modified to reflect the fact that exports contain imported components. When this is done, the relationship in export industries between employment created per unit of value-added (not gross value) may be more similar between Mexican and foreign firms than is now thought to be the case. This is recognized explicitly in the case of *maquiladora* industries, whose exports are reported as "services."

If the *maquiladora* program is not taken into account, if adjustments affecting labor created per unit of exports are not made, and if Mexican participation in ownership of multinational corporations is ignored, then it seems likely that as Mexican industrialization leads to expanded trade with the United States, then foreign-owned (probably U.S.) firms using capital-intensive production are likely to get more of the benefit from trade than are Mexican-owned firms using labor-intensive means of production (if industrialization in the 1980s and thereafter follows earlier patterns). Yet the National Industrial Development Plan indicates that export growth would be concentrated in oil and petrochemicals, automobiles, basic chemicals, metallic ores, commerce, shoes and clothing, electric machinery, agriculture, and basic metals. Of this group, petroleum and basic petrochemicals and some mining are reserved to the state; foreigners may own 34 to 49 percent of some mining activities and 40 percent of auto parts manufacturing. When not otherwise specified, foreign investment may hold no more than 49 percent of the capital of business enterprises.

Mexican industrialization seems likely to yield increased trade primarily for Mexican-owned firms in industries that largely use capital-intensive methods of production. Industrialization will probably lead to an increase of Mexican-made components in manufactured goods which are exported. The increase of labor-intensive exports is in large part determined by the course of the U.S. economy, which heavily influences the *maquiladora* program. It is again worth stressing that *maquiladora* exports are listed as services, since the combination of U.S. and Mexican law determines whether Mexican exports take the form of goods or services.

Nations who trade can exchange either goods, services, or factors of production. Until the 1960s, most trade theory dealt with the exchange of goods and focused on the effect on the balance of trade of movement of goods. When a nation ran a long-term deficit or surplus in its balance of trade, attention focused on the financing of the deficit through capital movements. The trade of services, called "invisible items," was less often discussed; it is probably harder to obtain data on foreigners' purchases of services than of goods, and services were not a very large share of trade until nations became rich. Similarly, the movement of labor across national boundaries was not well integrated into trade theory, even though remittances from persons working abroad helped to finance imports. Finally, payments for technology were not a major part of trade theory until developing nations made a concerted effort to produce high technology goods.

If there were no barriers to trade in goods, services, or factors of production and, also, if national security and development did not influence trade practices, then Mexico would export goods and services in which it has low marginal costs of production compared to the United States and would also export unskilled and semiskilled labor. The United States would export a different set of goods and services. For example, where Mexico has a comparative advantage in tourism, the United States has a comparative advantage in providing specialized education and medical care. The United States would export skilled labor and technology. In theory, the free flow of goods, services, and factors of production would lead to the most efficient use of resources and to the highest possible income for both nations.

In 1980 neither nation was willing to remove all impediments to the free flow of goods, services, and factors of production. Mexico liberalized much of its trade, but expected to protect its industry from unequal competition. The United States maintained its preference for liberal trade regimes but did not change its immigration system to make possible the unlimited free entry of Mexican workers on either a temporary or permanent basis. In 1980 there was strong pressure to regularize the status of Mexicans working in the United States and to place the negotiations over their status in the broader context of Mexican–U.S. trade relationships.

New Regimes for Mexican–U.S. Trade

The United States has increasingly been concerned with stabilization of its western hemisphere trade. Interest at first focused on Canada; the Canadian-American Auto Agreement of 1965 established free trade between the United States and Canada in automotive products, as long as it was carried out by American Motors, Chrysler, Ford, or General Motors. As a result of this agreement, Canada specialized in small, standardized cars while the United States specialized in auto parts and larger, more varied cars. U.S. workers obtained trade adjustment assistance as part of the agreement. The United States did not extend the benefits of the agreement to other trading partners. Canada extended duty-free treatment of products covered by the agreement to its other trade partners on a most-favored-nation basis and took other actions which threatened the agreement.

The bilateral agreement was criticized because its benefits were restricted to selected producers, with only indirect benefits for consumers. The absence of complementary agreement on what measures could be taken by either nation to obtain new investment in the auto industry threatened to end the agreement in the late 1970s.

Despite the criticism of the auto agreements act, the United States was convinced of the continuing importance of trade relations with Canada. The Trade Act of 1974 stated that it was the sense of Congress that the United States would enter into a trade agreement with Canada which would guarantee continued stability to the economies of both nations. In order to promote this stability, the President was authorized to initiate negotiations for a trade agreement with Canada to establish a free-trade area. By 1979 Congress was more insistent on such action and broadened its focus. The Trade Agreements Act of 1979 reiterated the provisions about potential agreements with Canada and went on to state that

> the President shall study the desirability of entering into trade agreements with countries in the northern portion of the western hemisphere to promote the economic growth of the United States and such countries and the mutual expansion of market opportunities and report . . . his findings and conclusions within 2 years after the date of enactment of this Act. The study shall include an examination of competitive opportunities and conditions of competition between such countries and the United States in the agricultural, energy, and other appropriate sectors.

The 1979 legislation does not mention the various forms such an agreement might take. These include a free-trade area, which has no barriers to trade within it, but do not include the establishment of a common external tariff; a customs union, which is a free-trade area with common external tariffs; a common market, which is a customs union in which barriers to the movement of labor and corporate investment have been abolished; an economic union, which is a common market with harmonized fiscal policies; and a monetary union, which is an economic union in which monetary policies of the members are harmonized. In practice, each of these stages of economic integration can include all products or selected products and can be produced by all industry, or, as in the Canadian-American Auto Agreement, only designated producers. Trade agreements can also include specified exchanges of products, services, and technology and can provide for the joint development of specified activities.

President Lopez Portillo has already ruled out a common market for all products between Mexico and the United States on the grounds that Mexico, as the smaller of the two, would be unlikely to obtain sufficient advantage from such an agreement. A common market in energy has been ruled out because it would limit Mexico's ability to use its oil in bilateral trade negotiations. At the same time, the United States' erratic handling of energy policy in the 1970s probably contributed to this decision.

The underlying premise in evaluating the regimes for Mexican–U.S. trade is that Mexico's first priority is the construction of a well-functioning market within Mexico, and that trade regimes will be evaluated according to the ways in which they enable Mexico to meet this goal. The use of broad trade regimes, ranging from a free-trade area to an economic union, would help some sectors of the economy. However, they would hurt others; the potential damage to Mexican industry from a nonselective elimination of barriers to trade made it necessary for the government to postpone consideration of establishing broad trade regimes. The government remained free to consider selective bilateral agreements and to take the many steps needed before any formal economic ties with the United States would be practical.

Mexican trade plans are linked to the achievement of targets set out in the National Industrial Development Plan. Mexico's overall economic growth rate is approximately that which was projected by the National Industrial Development Plan. However, in the late 1970s, many of the specific targets set forth in the voluntary Alliance for Production Agreements between government and industry were not met, in part due to shortages of inputs and transportation facilities as well as insufficiently attractive profits. In 1980 the government modified the Alliance for Production Agreement format: the new agreements between industry and government are binding, requiring industry to meet targets on time or lose incentives. The high level of profits in the Mexican economy in 1979 helped to make investment attractive.

An example of a new agreement, and its implications for trade policy, is the new agreement in food, which requires firms signing the agreement to use 25 percent of their production capacity for designated products. In exchange, the government guarantees the supply of raw materials, labeling, and packaging materials. Special credit lines are established, and free information services are provided to firms undertaking feasibility studies. Most of the products in question are price controlled.

Bilateral trade agreements which help to supply goods and services in short supply in Mexico, and which are needed under binding Alliance for Production Agreements, may well receive favorable consideration. Conversely, bilateral trade agreements cannot specify that Mexico import goods in which it hopes to become self-sufficient; foreigners will not be allowed to control essential supplies. For example, in 1980 the government auctioned the right to produce certain pharmaceuticals. Bidders were required to export, incorporate local products, limit their payments for technical assistance, and limit foreign equity to 40 to 49 percent. In exchange, the government offered fiscal incentives, cut-rate fuel, and access to preferential credit. Although foreigners can invest in pharmaceuticals, pharmaceutical industry growth in Mexico may limit imports of these goods. The government mentioned protection against imports by requiring an import license for products which the government wants to be produced in Mexico.

A bilateral trade agreement with the United States is also likely to include the export of goods produced in Mexican border and frontier zones, both because they are targeted for development in the National Industrial Development Plan and because the shortage of transportation and storage facilities in Mexico makes it difficult to export goods produced in the interior. Conversely, inclusion of imports from the United States of transportation and storage goods and services should be especially welcome, subject to the usual restrictions on foreign participation in Mexican industry.

It is also possible that a bilateral agreement with the United States would include Mexican export of crude oil in exchange for capital goods, technology, joint ventures, and joint research and development efforts—especially in the development of nontraditional fuels other than nuclear energy.

Maquiladoras are located in border areas and benefit from special Mexican legislation. New areas of the nation have been given free-zone status; priority areas for development have been given extensive benefits to stimulate new investment. Mexico has stated that the various regional benefits will be unified; bilateral trade agreements will be shaped to accommodate Mexico's regional development priorities. It is plausible that a gradual widening of the free zone, as well as overland smuggling of Mexico's underpriced gasoline and of United States' inexpensive goods, will lead to the establishment of a de facto Mexican–U.S. free-trade area.

The Canadian-American Auto Agreement is not likely to serve as a model for bilateral agreements between the United States and Mexico. An agreement restricting trade to specified firms would probably be acceptable if the Mexican and U.S. firms were of equal size. Large U.S. firms are often multinationals and are especially subject to political attack. Large Mexican firms often are wholly or partly owned by the Mexican government. Equal size of trade partners may require participation of a state-owned firm in such an agreement. Mexico may also want to include some small- and medium-scale firms in a bilateral trade agreement covering an industry.

The United States, on the other hand, has long feared state ownership and foreign influence in the U.S. economy. A bilateral trade agreement which includes a state-owned firm, therefore, may not be acceptable.

Both the United States and Mexico wish to protect their workers; if it is administratively feasible, both nations may want to stipulate the local content of the goods covered by the treaty to ensure that the goods are provided by firms and workers located within Mexico or the United States. Both nations would be discouraged from purchasing components from third parties, assembling them, and then labeling them as "of national origin" for purposes of a bilateral trade treaty.

It should again be stressed that since Mexico uses bilateral trade agreements to develop its economy as well as to promote trade, factors of production are included in its bilateral trade agreements. Thus, in 1980, Mexico suggested that its trade partners draw up bilateral agreements for joint ventures for telecommunications, petrochemicals, mining, port infrastructure, steel, fishing, metallic products, naval construction, cellulose and paper, energy-generating equipment, chemicals, tourism, and projects in participation with medium-size Mexican investors. Increased access of Mexico to foreign capital markets for investment and financing of Mexican imports appears to go hand-in-hand with the proposed bilateral agreements, although the financial measures are published separately. In exchange for joint ventures and financing, trade partners hope for increased supplies of Mexican oil, either for consumption or for refining and marketing to other nations.

Given Mexico's wish for diversity of trade and investment partners, a package which spreads U.S. investment among many sectors, rather than concentrating a large amount in a single sector, is likely to be emphasized.

The negotiations over such a package will pose problems for the United States. The government cannot commit private industry investment funds, as the Alliance for Progress amply demonstrated in the 1960s. Similarly, Secretary of Energy Schlesinger's 1977 veto of the purchase of Mexican natural gas indicates that businessmen cannot operate in the absence of detailed knowledge of government policy. A Mexican–U.S. bilateral trade treaty which includes the commitment of funds to specific investment projects will require the United States to increase the coordination and cooperation between business and government and will raise issues of how to ensure compliance by private enterprise with government treaties as economic conditions change.

As financial measures gradually become linked to trade agreements, the United States may press for the reporting to the U.S. government of interest earned on deposits held by Americans in Mexico. Although light taxes are paid to the Mexican government, interest earned on deposits in Mexico, when not reported to the U.S. government, is almost tax free compared to that earned on deposits in the United States. Regulation of the flow of factors of production would increase the U.S. government's tax receipts.

Regulation of the flow of factors of production includes government responsibility for the flow of labor between the two nations. Part of the difficulty in controlling the flow of labor from northern Mexico to the United States reflects the fact that many people leaving Mexico for the United States are not Mexicans, but come from Central and South America. Mexico apparently does not wish to take responsibility for them and also wishes to ensure that the benefits of Mexico's oil wealth go to Mexicans, rather than to other Latin Americans attracted by Mexico's improving prospects. As a result, in 1980 the government announced that it would implement a national identity card system. This could be used in a system where the number of laborers and their skills made available to the United States were regulated by a treaty covering temporary immigrants in the hope that working conditions offered laborers with treaty protection would be better than those obtained by illegal entrants, recently called "undocumented aliens."

It has been suggested that Mexican migrants who enter illegally in fact do work that U.S. citizens will not perform and also that they contribute to tax and social security systems from which they will draw fewer benefits than U.S. workers. On the other hand, U.S. workers claim that they either do not obtain jobs or are paid lower wages because cheap labor from Mexico is available. In addition, it has been suggested that admission of Mexican workers be handled in the same way as the admission of goods: where damage to a union or a group of U.S. workers can be shown, compensation similar to trade adjustment assistance payments should be given. Similarly, where migrants' use of school and hospital facilities poses a financial burden, the federal government should be required to provide at least a share of the costs; no locality should pay all of the costs of a program whose benefits accrue to the nation.

Labor regulation should cover the increased flow of labor from the United States to Mexico. Retired U.S. citizens and those with specialized skills needed for the implementation of the National Industrial Development Plan would be able to help Mexico to meet its development goals. They would also benefit from policies which would make it easier for them to work on a temporary basis in Mexico. Including both Mexicans working in the U.S. and U.S. citizens working in Mexico in a single treaty should make it easier for both nations to work out mutually acceptable solutions to migration questions by providing a framework in which both sides comment on proposed legislation affecting their citizens before it is enacted. In the absence of this framework, delicate questions of foreign influence on domestic legislation governing immigrants could be raised if prior consultation were offered.

In time, Mexican–U.S. bilateral trade agreements may be expanded to include exchange of educational and training opportunities, provision of nonbanking financial services, and other highly specialized service activities.

Mexico's industrialization plans and trade prospects will lead to increased trade and economic growth for both Mexico and the United States. Mexico's clearly expressed preference for bilateral trade regimes is one of many factors that will tend to shift U.S. policy preference from general to specific trade agreements abroad and to economic policy measures which have an openly acknowledged selective impact on the domestic economy, in the hope that they will fight inflation, ensure supplies, and permit the sustained economic growth of both nations.

Al R. Wichtrich

4

Mexican-American
Commercial Relations

Trading and Investment Environment

To understand U.S.–Mexican trade and U.S. investment in Mexico, it is imperative to have some knowledge of the environment in which these two vital functions have operated over the years. To a greater or lesser degree, trade and investment have always been at the vortex of U.S.–Mexican relations. They bring into sharp focus, or spin off in vague imagery, facets of our relationship that at times appear strained and other times cordial, reflected at different times in many different opinions in both countries.

Our trading relations are complex and puzzling. There are, however, certain dominant characteristics that are woven in and out of trade and investment patterns, practically all of which bear the stamp of history.

One such characteristic is that most Mexicans have an inherent

AL R. WICHTRICH *is director-at-large and special advisor to the president of the American Chamber of Commerce of Mexico. Previously he was president and president-counselor of that organization. Mr. Wichtrich is also a member of the board of several Mexican-American civic organizations in Mexico City. He has thirty-four years of experience in the Latin American business world, thirty of which have been spent in Mexico.*

mistrust of U.S. government trade policies toward Mexico. Two examples illustrate this point. Mexico did not initially embrace the Generalized System of Preferences (GSP) as prescribed by the U.S. Trade Act of 1974, even though the benefits to Mexico were great. The qualifications for receiving GSP benefits, such as not belonging to a cartel or to OPEC, seemed to run contrary to the Echeverría U.N. proposal of the Charter of Economic Rights and Duties of Nations, and therefore GSP was perceived by some key people in the Mexican government as a U.S. attempt to divide Latin American countries and thereby weaken unity among Third World nations.

And again, Mexico has declared that for the present it will not join the General Agreement on Trade and Tariffs (GATT), in spite of having negotiated very favorable terms for entry into GATT. (This point will be discussed later.) During the public debate on the question, the U.S. position, which was that it wanted Mexico to join GATT, was highlighted. The U.S. perception of the benefits Mexico would receive from joining GATT were explained only in general terms. The fact that the U.S. favored Mexico joining GATT was seen by many Mexicans as a U.S. ploy, and therefore not to be trusted. Reinforcing this feeling was the sense that, had Mexico decided to join GATT, it would have appeared to be bowing to U.S. pressure. For political reasons, this would not have been acceptable.

Another dominant Mexican notion affecting U.S.–Mexican commerce is that the U.S. is perceived to have imperialistic designs. This perception is brought about by a historical focus reflected in teachings in all public schools. Stress is placed on the loss of Mexican territory to the U.S., the invasion of Mexico in 1847, and the presence of U.S. Marines in Veracruz as late as 1914. Economic and political domination by foreign powers over the last four hundred years is a vivid reminder to the Mexicans of the importance of maintaining their trading and investment options open and independent of any foreign power, particularly the U.S.

As a consequence, the Mexican government is fearful, almost to an extreme, of being dependent on the U.S. Although current trading relations between our two countries are viewed by more mature individuals as being in the mutual interest of both countries, there are groups in Mexico, largely of leftist tinge, that are still quite vocal on the subject of dependency. Formulation of Mexican trade policy toward the U.S. has to contend with this underlying fact. Perhaps the most recent illustration is the sale of Mexican gas to the U.S. The

Mexican government's original willingness to sell gas to the U.S. at a specified price overrode a wave of public opinion generated by more extreme elements who believed Mexico would become dependent on the U.S. because the U.S. would be Mexico's only customer. Subsequent events unfortunately gave credence to the advocates of "nondependence" and caused considerable embarrassment to the President of Mexico. The U.S. did not approve the initial sale price, and it was not until after bruised relations that Mexico and the U.S. agreed much later on a pricing formula.

The problems resulting from the domination in trading relationships by an industrialized, developed economy over an underdeveloped or developing economy, have been debated in world, regional, and local forums ever since UNCTAD I (U.N. Conference on Trade and Development) of sixteen years ago. This has led the Third World nations, originally a group of seventy-seven, to seek formulas for more rapid economic development of the lesser developed countries (LDCs). One of the reasons these nations continue to lag behind the industrialized countries is the nature of their exports and imports. In very simplistic terms, the LDCs export basic raw materials to industrialized nations and import manufactured or processed goods at much higher total prices, thereby suffering a chronic deficit in their balance of payments.

In the case of Mexican–U.S. trade relations, a close analysis of Mexican exports and imports (excluding the export of petroleum and petroleum products) reveals Mexico's current underlying policy of switching from exports of raw materials to manufactured and semi-manufactured goods. Philosophy and legislation aim at implementing this policy. Mexican–U.S. trading relations are exacerbated by the concept of the relationship as being between the "powerful rich neighbor" to the north and the "poor weak neighbor" to the south. This has been described by clichés such as "poor Mexico—so far from God and so close to the United States," or "Mexico would rather be the head of a mouse than the tail of a lion." Mexico feels that the U.S. pays only lip service to the "neighbor concept" and is not aware of, or sensitive to, Mexico's legitimate aspirations. Their purchases from the U.S., they insist, should entitle Mexico to greater access to U.S. markets. This would stimulate the Mexican economy, create more jobs, and—as a consequence and in the mutual benefit of both countries—cement a strong, friendly trade relationship. Based on this perception, U.S. nontariff trade barriers, quotas, protectionist legislation, and antidumping charges are seen as measures to keep Mexico dependent on the U.S.

In summary, general mistrust of the United States as an imperialist nation, Mexico's intense desire not to become dependent on the U.S., and Mexico's sense of being an unequal trading partner and neighbor of the U.S. contribute to a large degree to the formation of the trade and investment environment between Mexico and the U.S.

The U.S. reaction to Mexican charges is that the Mexicans want to have their cake and eat it too, that our trading relations are inter-dependent, multilateral, and in mutual interest. If Mexico wishes more access to the U.S. market, it should allow greater access to the Mexican market for U.S. imports.

Trade Statistics: What They Show

In 1970, 60 percent of Mexican exports were to the U.S., and 64 percent of Mexican imports were from the U.S. (see tables). Some ten

TABLE 1.   U.S. TRADE WITH MEXICO *

Year	U.S. Exports	U.S. Imports **	Share of Imports Supplied by the U.S.***	Share of Exports Shipped to the U.S.***
	(Millions of dollars)		(Percent)	
1970	1,704	1,218	64	60
1971	1,620	1,262	61	62
1972	1,982	1,633	60	68
1973	2,937	2,306	60	63
1974	4,856	3,391	62	54
1975	5,160	3,060	63	58
1976	5,002	3,599	63	57
1977	4,822	4,694	64	66
1978	6,680	6,196	61	68
1979	9,847 **	8,996	62	68

* According to U.S. trade data, Mexico in 1979 was the fourth most important market for U.S. goods following Canada, $33 billion; Japan, $17 billion; the United Kingdom, $10 billion; Mexico, $9,847 billion; and West Germany, $8.4 billion.

** *Source:* U.S. Department of Commerce. Statistics include U.S. exports to and imports from Mexican in-bond industries (*maquiladoras*) and U.S.–Mexican frontier trade.

*** *Source:* Banco de México, which excludes data on *maquiladora* trade with the U.S. and frontier trade, principally with the U.S.

years later Mexican exports to the United States were 68 percent of its total exports, and imports from the U.S. were 62 percent of its total imports. The value of total Mexican exports in 1970 was $1.3 billion, and 60 percent of this amount (or $742 million) went to the U.S. Some ten years later the U.S. market imported 68 percent of total Mexican exports, a major percentage increase. The dollar volume of Mexican exports to the U.S. jumped from $742 million to $6.1 billion in ten years, whereas total world Mexican exports rose from $1.2 billion to almost $9 billion.

Mexican imports from the U.S. in dollar volume in 1970 were 64 percent of all Mexico's imports and amounted to $1.7 billion. Ten years later the percentage of Mexican imports from the U.S. was 62 percent. The dollar volume increased to $7.6 billion, and Mexican total imports went from $2.3 to $12 billion.

TABLE 1A.   MEXICO'S GENERAL FOREIGN TRADE PATTERNS

Imports	1979, $12,097 million; 1978, $8,143 million; U.S. share 1979, 62 percent; Japan, 6 percent; West Germany, 6 percent; France, 2 percent.
Major imports	Industrial machinery, automobile assembly parts, organic chemical products, iron and steel products, precision instruments, grains.
Exports	1979, $8,913 million; 1978, $6,217 million; U.S. share 1979, 68 percent; Spain, 5 percent; Israel, 3 percent; Japan, 3 percent; West Germany, 3 percent.
Major exports	Crude oil, coffee, cotton, assorted machinery, shrimp.

In summary, statistics on the volume of U.S.–Mexican trade demonstrate that the U.S. share of the Mexican market remains more or less constant, but that dollar volume increases in a very significant degree to the extent that Mexico was by mid-1980 our third trading partner. The total dollar volume of trade between Mexico and the United States rose from $2.9 billion in 1970 to $19 billion in 1979. This represents 66.8 percent and 65 percent respectively of *total* Mexican trade.

The trade deficit with the United States in 1970 was $530 million, rising to $1.6 billion in 1979. However, Mexico enjoyed a slight surplus in its trade with the U.S. in the first quarter of 1980. The highest trade deficit registered with the United States was $2.3 billion in 1975.

Trade figures of 1978 and 1979 are indicative of the rapid trade expansion between the United States and Mexico. In 1978 Mexico imported almost $6.7 billion, and in 1979 this volume rose 46 percent to $9.8 billion. Mexican exports increased 46 percent, from $6.4 billion in 1978 to $8.9 billion in 1979.

It is interesting to note that, of total Mexican imports from the U.S. in 1978 and 1979, 24 percent ($1.2 billion) and 28 percent ($2.1 billion), respectively, represented imports of capital goods. As we will see later, this fact had an impact on the investment climate.

Mexico's percentage of its total exports to the U.S. in the last few years is altered by exports of crude oil and gas. This is demonstrated by $2.4 billion total exports in 1977, of which crude was $832 million, a leap of $4.4 billion in total exports in 1978, of which crude rose to $1.5 billion, and $6.1 billion total export in 1979, of which crude was $3.38 billion. The percentage of crude exports in dollar volume to total exports in dollar volume was 34 percent in 1977, 34 percent in 1978, and 49 percent in 1979. Thus, for the years 1977 and 1978, traditional Mexican exports to the U.S. represented 66 percent of the total, but for 1979 this was reduced to 51 percent.

Mexico has had a chronic trade deficit with the United States. In 1979, as mentioned, this deficit was $1.5 billion. While there are prospects that, on an annual basis, Mexico might have an overall trade surplus with the U.S. as of 1980, this would depend largely on the volume of petroleum and gas exports and their prices.

Petroleum and gas exports to the U.S. will continue to distort the Mexican economic picture. A movement from a trade deficit to a trade surplus with the U.S. and an ever increasing positive balance of payments place Mexico in the category of an advanced developing country. South Korea, Brazil, and Taiwan are also in this category.

Although statistics are placing Mexico in a league with some developed economies, these figures are misleading. Imports of agricultural commodities and capital goods, unemployment figures, and low

TABLE 2A. VALUE OF MEXICO'S PRINCIPAL IMPORTS (THOUSANDS OF U.S. DOLLARS)

	1978 *	1979 *	1979 Percent of Total **	Absolute Change **	Percentage Change †
TOTAL (CIF)	1,143,701	12,907,231	100	3,953,530	48.5
Freight and insurance	419,121	599,812	4	180,691	43.1
Commercial value	7,724,580	11,497,419	96	3,772,839	48.8
A. Consumption goods	427,083	678,254	5	251,171	58.8
B. Production goods	7,297,497	10,819,165	89	3,521,668	48.3
1. Goods of intermediate use	5,316,113	7,411,885	61	2,095,772	39.4
Animal and vegetable oils, foods, drinks	645,032	77,405	0	132,273	20.5
Energy sources	202,605	245,972	2	43,367	21.4
Textiles	36,838	70,554	0	33,716	91.5
Paper	121,683	193,438	1	71,775	59.0
Chemicals	977,789	1,383,583	11	406,794	41.5
Transport equipment	728,122	994,551	8	266,429	36.6
Steel	913,316	1,115,258	9	201,942	22.1
Other industries	1,238,827	1,862,453	15	623,626	50.3
Other goods of intermediate use	451,901	768,671	6	316,770	70.1
2. Investment goods	1,981,384	3,407,280	28	1,425,896	72.0
Machinery and apparatus	1,510,463	2,542,813	21	1,032,350	68.3
Tools and instruments	209,091	352,070	2	144,979	70.0
Transport	102,812	264,768	2	161,956	157.5
Other investment goods	161,018	247,629	2	86,611	53.8

* Preliminary figures.
** Subtotals vary from 100 percent due to rounding.
† 1979 compared to 1978.
Source: Banco de México Indicadores Económicas, January 1980.

TABLE 2B. VALUE OF MEXICO'S PRINCIPAL EXPORTS †† (THOUSANDS OF U.S. DOLLARS)

	1978 *	1979 *	1979 Percent of Total **	Absolute Change †	Percentage Change †
TOTAL	6,217,340	8,913,287	100	2,695,947	43.4
A. *Primary activities*	3,490,887	5,852,096	65	2,391,209	68.5
Agriculture, forestry, fishing	1,502,791	1,777,820	19	275,029	18.3
Extractive industries	1,988,096	4,104,276	46	2,116,180	106.4
Crude petroleum	1,773,604	3,789,261	42	2,015,657	113.6
B. *Transformation industries*	2,726,453	3,031,191	34	304,738	11.2
Food and drinks	678,525	750,067	8	71,542	10.5
Textiles, clothing, shoes	165,383	180,808	2	25,425	16.4
Chemicals	311,947	450,467	5	138,520	44.4
Steel	68,497	65,692	0	2,805	4.1
Machinery and transport equipment	592,946	597,358	6	4,412	0.7
Other industries	919,155	986,799	11	67,644	7.4

* Preliminary figures.
** Subtotals vary from 100 percent due to rounding.
† 1979 compared to 1978.
†† Excludes *maquiladora* operations.
Source: Banco de México Indicadores Económicas, January 1980.

exports of nonhydrocarbons (such as manufactured and semimanufactured goods) are more typical of less developed economies. U.S.–
Mexican trade relations also must be examined not only by con-
templating trade figures, but also by examining in depth the general
overall real economic development picture in Mexico.

Although Mexico's total exports rose 45.5 percent from 1978 to
1979, crude oil accounted for almost half of this increase, and nonoil
exports increased by only 13.3 percent. The composition of U.S.–
Mexican trade seems to change constantly (though, as mentioned before, the percentages of imports and exports remain more or less the
same). For example, Mexico's top exports in 1979 were crude oil,
coffee, frozen shrimp, chemical products, cotton, automotive vehicles,
parts and components, electrical and electromechanical machinery
and equipment, tomatoes, fresh vegetables, and cattle on the hoof.
In contrast, ten to fifteen years ago, most of Mexico's exports would
be classified as traditional: sugar, coffee, cotton, lead, copper, and
zinc.

In the case of petroleum, it was not until 1975 that Mexico showed
a favorable balance of trade in this category. A dramatic example is
shown in the import figures of 1974, where imports of petroleum and
petroleum products amounted to $382 million. Current figures show
the complete reversal of this trend. In the case of sugar, Mexico,
which was an exporter, is now an importer. Cotton and coffee still
remain as large export items, as well as copper, lead, and zinc. Fresh
tomatoes, strawberries, melons, and winter vegetables also loom large
as exports to the U.S. Nontraditional exports, such as manufactured
and semimanufactured goods, are the result of Mexican government
policy to shift as rapidly as possible from exports of basic raw materials to manufactured goods.

As stated, in spite of changes in the U.S.–Mexican trading pan-
orama, the U.S. share of the Mexican market and the Mexican share
of exports (excluding hydrocarbons) to the U.S. remain more or less
constant. How long the U.S. will be able to maintain this preponderance in trade with Mexico is difficult to determine. As Mexican
imports increase along with its 8 percent gross domestic product
(GDP) growth rate, competition for a larger share of this growing
market is becoming very keen. It is my belief that the U.S. will be
hard-pressed to maintain its share of the Mexican market if it con-

tinues to do business in the "same old way." The British, Germans, French, Japanese, Italians, and some nations of the Socialist bloc countries are all competing for this market. They are shrewd traders who compete with financial packages and are aided by their governments. U.S. exporters, on the other hand, are sometimes hampered on a world-wide basis by our own laws in securing orders. One good example is the inability of the Eximbank (Export-Import Bank) to lend to a country accused of violating human rights.

Over the last decades, while Mexico has been one of the four or five largest trading partners of the U.S., it has always had a trade deficit with the U.S. Within a world context, Mexico was in a preferred geographical position for trade with the U.S. Also, more recently, with the peso riding with the dollar, European or Japanese goods have become more costly.

The U.S. attitude toward trade with Mexico seems to be one of benign neglect—an attitude not in the best interest of either country. Mexico does not want her trade relations with the U.S. to be taken for granted and is constantly striving to diversify by trading more extensively with other countries. Mexico's major trading partners, after the United States, are Spain, Israel, Japan, West Germany, France, and Brazil. While the U.S. enjoys the major share, developing trade with other oil-importing countries will surely have an impact on future Mexican–U.S. trade.

In April of 1980, Mexico's daily crude exports were averaging as follows: U.S., 572,000 barrels; Spain, 60,000; Israel, 45,000; Brazil, 20,000; and Costa Rica, 7,500. By year's end, daily crude exports were estimated as: U.S., 733,000; Spain, 160,000; Israel, 45,000; and Japan, 100,000; plus some shipments to France, Sweden, Brazil, Canada, and Costa Rica. PEMEX reached exports of 1,040,000 barrels per day (B/D) in late March of 1980.

Japan continues to negotiate with Mexico for oil exports of 300,-000 B/D, and Mexico has completed an agreement with Canada to ship 50,000 B/D, as well as to export 10,000 B/D to Jamaica.

Mexican policy is to utilize its nonrenewable resources (petroleum); to develop renewable resources, such as an industrial base that will allow Mexico to manufacture capital goods; and to compete favorably in the world market. Until this happens, Mexico will continue to import vast amounts of machinery, in part to satisfy PEMEX demands, as well as the needs of the private and public sectors to satisfy the annual development goals. Other renewable resources to be developed are the fishing industry, tourism, and agriculture.

Mexico's needs for the immediate future are staggering. As Mexico is able to meet its economic goals, however, the need to import will lessen, and exports should increase. At the present time almost 100 percent of the production of the economy goes to meet domestic demands, and the ability to export industrial goods is largely marginal. The exception to this is the automotive industry, which by government decree must export to generate sufficient foreign exchange to compensate for the cost of its imports. This will be discussed in greater detail in the section dealing with foreign investment.

In summary, Mexico's trade with the U.S. and the rest of the world is expanding rapidly as a result of development of its oil industry, liberalization of trading conditions, and 8 percent GDP growth.

Trade Legislation and Other Recent Changes

In 1977 Mexico began to eliminate the requirement of import permits. This represented a significant change in a heretofore rigid protectionist policy, under which all imports, with but few exceptions, required permits. Requests for permits were subject to bureaucratic obstacles and delays. The main problem was to secure permission to import a product when the approval had to come from a commission made up of Mexican businessmen who manufactured a similar product.

This nontariff trade barrier is gradually being eliminated, and at this writing approximately 72 percent of the items on tariff schedules do not require prior import permits. The remaining 28 percent, however, represent approximately 55 percent of the volume. Nevertheless, this is a significant step in the right direction toward liberalizing trade. A high tariff, sometimes substituted for a prior import permit, is negotiable, according to market conditions, and this allows protection to an industry for only a specified period until it becomes competitive. It also allows the import of goods considered luxury items, for example, luxury automobiles not manufactured in Mexico which heretofore were not importable regardless of duties.

Another recent change was the customs valuation decree. The purpose was to eliminate discrepancies in the values of similar merchandise for customs purposes, and thus eliminate unfair competition among importers of similar merchandise from different countries. The decree allows the customs "evaluator" to determine the fair value of the merchandise being imported regardless of the value shown on the invoice.

Mexico continues to give fiscal and other incentives to stimulate exports, and in some cases these incentives have triggered countervailing duty charges in the U.S. Antidumping, countervailing duties, and GATT will be explained later.

The U.S. legislation which affects Mexican–U.S. trade is the Trade Act of 1979 and its modifications to the Generalized System of Preferences. This also is pertinent to conducting U.S.–Mexican trade on a bilateral as opposed to multilateral basis. The Trade Act of 1979 should not have any great impact on U.S.–Mexican trade, as long as the United States continues to concede to Mexico a most-favored-nation status.

Mexico's unwillingness to become a signatory of GATT at this time does produce an unfavorable impact on Mexican–U.S. trade in two areas.

1. Mexico will lose approximately $536 million in tariff concessions previously negotiated with the U.S. as an annex to the Mexican protocol of accession to GATT. Negotiated were $304 million of industrial products and $232 million in agricultural concessions. Both countries now consider this agreement invalid.

2. Because Mexico is not a member of GATT, any countervailing duties charges against Mexico will not have to demonstrate major injury to the U.S. party making such charges. It now becomes necessary only to prove that Mexico is selling a product in the U.S. which is subsidized. This normally is quite easy to prove, whereas to prove that Mexican subsidized exports to the U.S. are a major cause of injury to a company or a sector of industry is most difficult.

Mexico's decision not to become a signatory of GATT at this time is probably the most significant act by the Mexican government affecting Mexican–U.S. trade in recent years. It serves to underscore that historical actions color current U.S. relations and that trade and investment relations are often at the root of overall Mexican–U.S. relations.

The reactions in Mexico and the U.S. to the former's position on GATT are worth mentioning. In the U.S. initial surprise turned into a feeling of injury and subsequent anger, which fortunately subsided to a more mature attitude of "let's wait and see." In Mexico it was viewed as a victory for the advocates of nationalism. Third World philosophies, economic independence, and for those who generally mistrust U.S. motives.

Opinion leaders in Mexico and the U.S. concede that the reasons for not joining GATT are political. The President of Mexico stated that "the advantages are more apparent than real," adding that

> negotiations for assurance of basic supplies by contracting parties is one of the issues that worries us most. Because of their terms and in relation to our world energy plan proposed before the United Nations, we consider that the rules liberalizing trade are not adequate to promote a more just world economic order, and that the certainty and objectives of our world plan would be endangered, with possible variances in supply to contracting parties, and so we prefer to advance in the concept of a new, more just economic order, even if we have to resort, outside of GATT, to bilateral negotiations, as we have done up to now.

Whatever the real reasons for Mexico not joining GATT, it is quite evident that Mexican–U.S. trade will now and in the foreseeable future be conducted on a bilateral basis. At the present time there are no bilateral general trade agreements between the U.S. and Mexico. The bilateral trade agreement of 1942 was denounced in 1956 by Mexico, and the much heralded agreement announced in the winter of 1976 still remains in limbo, with neither side taking the necessary legal steps to ratify and make the treaty binding.

The consultative mechanism established in 1977 by mutual accord of Presidents Carter and Lopez Portillo to bring about a continuous review of Mexican–U.S. relations, of which the working group on trade is a part, becomes even more significant on matters relating to bilateral trade. Most of our trading relations with Mexico are de facto bilateral. Multifiber textile exports to the U.S. are under a multilateral agreement in the sense that Mexico shares the U.S. global textile quota with other countries in the world. From Mexico's perspective, however, it is bilateral. Mexico's exports of winter vegetables, such as tomatoes, melons, strawberries, asparagus, and eggplant, go almost exclusively to the U.S. and are dependent on U.S. market conditions. Another example of bilateral trade with the U.S. is the tourist industry. Approximately 80 percent of all tourists visiting Mexico are Americans, a logical consequence of the proximity of the U.S. to Mexico. Yet another is the latest bilateral air agreement, which allows U.S. and Mexican airlines a greater number of flights to key areas in the U.S. and Mexico. The Mexican government recognizes the importance of the tourism industry and the need for developing new tourist areas and more hotel rooms. A strong factor here is the peso-dollar parity and its relation to other tourist areas, such as Japan and Europe.

The magnitude of this industry is demonstrated by the nearly $1.5 billion spent by foreign tourists in Mexico in 1979. Mexican tourists spent almost $700 million, mostly in the U.S., leaving Mexico a favorable balance of payment for this category of $800 million.

Another bilateral trade area is in the so-called "border transaction," commercial operations that take place within a limited zone of both countries and are usually limited to the border cities, such as Mexicali (Mexico) and Calexico (California), Nogales (Mexico) and Nogales (Arizona), Ciudad Juárez (Mexico) and El Paso (Texas). In 1979 Mexico received almost $3 billion for transactions on its side of the border, and the communities on the U.S. side of the border received approximately $2.5 billion, leaving Mexico a favorable balance of payments of $500 million.

The "in-bond" industries, known also as *maquiladoras,* "twin plants," "production sharing," etc., are located for the most part along the Mexican side of the U.S.–Mexico border. These plants assemble component parts that are reexported to the U.S., and because of the provisions of articles 806.30 and 807.00 of the Customs Code, are subject to duty only on the value added by the operation in Mexico. These are labor-intensive industries and create sorely needed jobs in Mexico. This concept is not limited to Mexico, for it is found in LDCs where wage rates offer a comparative advantage. In the case of Mexico, there are 619 "in-bond" plants employing close to 120,000 persons. The commercial activities of these 120,000 employees and 619 "in-bond" plants contribute to a great extent to the economic impact of border transactions. The value added to the assembled components returned to the U.S. is estimated at $1.3 billion for 1980. Discrepancies in trade figures between the U.S. and Mexico may be attributed to the fact that Mexico does not include "in-bond" imports and exports in her trade figures, whereas the U.S. does.

Although "in-bond" operations are conducted all over the world and utilize component parts from wherever it is most economically desirable, in the case of the U.S. and Mexico it takes on a status of bilateral trade, in that U.S. components are assembled in Mexico, jobs are created, and the assembled product is reexported to the U.S.

Other bilateral commercial operations not recognized because of their irregular nature include the remittances made by undocumented Mexican aliens to their families in Mexico—a sum estimated to run into the billions of dollars.

The drug traffic between Mexico and the U.S. is also believed to involve billions of dollars, and contraband still continues to flourish from the United States to Mexico and is another multibillion dollar trade item. So it appears that Mexico can proceed with some degree of certainty on the assumption that bilateral trade with the U.S. will continue to expand, and that Mexico's decision to remain outside of GATT will not impair U.S.–Mexican trade, at least not as much as suggested at first.

The GSP is a framework whereby underdeveloped countries that are not members of OPEC and did not participate in the oil embargo against the U.S. or do not belong to some form of cartel can export to the United States duty free some 2,700 categories of products. Its purpose is to boost the economies of LDCs by encouraging exporters to find new markets for their products in the U.S. If a product qualifies for preferential treatment, it is allowed to enter the U.S. duty free.

The GSP was initiated in January 1976 and will terminate on January 4, 1985. Mexico was initially skeptical of its purpose and exported only $245 million under GSP in 1976. Later, as the benefits of GSP were better understood, exports rose to $368 million in 1977, $458 million in 1978, and more than $545 million in 1979.

A product may be eliminated from the GSP list if it loses its need for concessions, that is, if imports of the product from a single country exceed a certain dollar volume. In 1978 the cutoff limit was $37.3 million ($41 million for 1979). Future limits will continue to be adjusted according to the increase in the U.S. GNP.

Another criterion to determine the eligibility of a product on the GSP list is whether a country has supplied more than half of the total U.S. imports of that product for the prior year. In the case of

Mexico, exports of cauliflower to the U.S. of $35,000 in 1978 made that product ineligible for GSP treatment, because $35,000 represented more than half of total U.S. imports of cauliflower for that year. In another case Mexico supplied over 50 percent of railroad cars to the U.S., because during that year Canada did not export any to the U.S.

The Trade Agreement Act of 1979 amended the 1974 basic GSP statute, however, to allow for a presidential waiver if the import of a particular product exceeded the 50 percent criterion, but the total value of the category imported was less than $1 million.

Trade with the U.S. under GSP is expected to increase in forth-coming years, even though GSP is to terminate in January of 1985. There may be a slackening of interest, inasmuch as one of the criticisms against GSP was that it did not allow for long-range planning of new investment to manufacture eligible products.

U.S. Direct Private Foreign Investment in Mexico

Five years of World War II devastated much of the world and left large masses of consumers in need of goods and services. The United States began exporting goods and services to the rest of the world, and U.S. corporations began investing overseas, giving validity to the old saying that investment follows trade.

After 1945 the United States became the number one capital-exporting country. According to *Survey of Current Business,* October 1949, U.S. direct private foreign investment world-wide was $8.854 billion, mostly in Europe, Canada, Japan, and Australia, with very little in Latin America. The benchmark year for U.S. direct private investment in Mexico is 1950, with approximately $390 million, whereas world-wide U.S. investment was $12 billion.

Estimates for new U.S. direct investment in Mexico for 1980 amount to a little over $1 billion, which brings the total to $6.3 billion. *Survey of Current Business* of the U.S. Department of Commerce indicates that 88 percent of the new investment is in manufacturing. Accumulated U.S. direct private investment in Mexico represents about 4 percent of total national investment and about 9 percent of total private investment. It still represents only about 2 percent of total U.S. investment overseas.

Mexican Development Plans and Foreign Investment

Mexico's National Industrial Development Plan was created in March 1979 to facilitate dynamic, orderly, and steady economic growth and serves as a basis for economic development through 1990. It takes into account Mexico's new petroleum wealth, the need to create employment, and the need to correct weaknesses of the economic structure which have persisted since World War II.

One weakness was that production focused on substitution of consumer goods imports (which meant that industry depended largely on the domestic market), raw materials were insufficiently exploited, and equipment and intermediate goods were imported, in turn contributing to Mexico's imbalance of payments. As the industrial activity of Mexico increased, the per capita income of the Mexican population rose and so did Mexican imports, which caused the trade gap to widen. Mining, agriculture, and tourism at first covered the trade imbalance, but they were unable to keep the trade gap closed. In order to maintain industrial growth rates, it was necessary to increase the foreign debt.

It was because of import substitution that U.S. direct private foreign investment entered Mexico, largely in the fields of consumer goods. As recently as fifteen years ago Mexico monitored imports, and when these reached a level that merited the installation of a factory, Mexico would give incentives to such an investment, consisting of prohibition of further imports of that particular item. As foreign debt increased, Mexico became more dependent on foreign sources for imports; these in turn were substituted by new industries, either foreign or national, creating more imports.

Mexico's oil wealth is producing greater financial independence, enabling Mexico to begin to attack one of its most serious economic ills—unemployment. One of the goals of the National Industrial Development Plan is to eradicate unemployment by the end of this century. In order to reach the objectives of its new economic strategy, Mexico must do the following:

1. reorient production toward basic consumer goods,
2. develop high-productivity areas able to export and efficiently substitute imports,

3. make better use of Mexico's natural resources,
4. decentralize economic activity, and
5. link big business with medium and small business.

As mentioned in the section concerning trade, Mexico must not be content to be an exporter of crude oil only. Nonrenewable resources must be converted to renewable resources in order to create permanent sources of employment by adding value to basic renewable raw materials. This policy affects Mexican–U.S. trade, as well as U.S. investment in Mexico. Promotion of employment and exports, support for small business, and geographic decentralization of industry will be followed within priorities based on geographical areas and industrial sectors. At the top of the list of priorities is the industrial processing of agricultural products and the manufacture of capital goods.

A coordinated procurement program in the public sector, tax incentives, reduced energy rates and tariffs, preferential rates on loans, and new sources of capital will serve as inducement for business to enter priority industrial sectors and the geographical area designated by the government. As it relates to foreign investment, the plan offers substantial incentives in the area of taxes, government purchasing, differential rates on energy, and protective measures such as tariffs. Benefiting from these incentives assumes obligations regarding the amount of investment, scale of plan, location in priority areas, production goals, Mexican integration, pricing, and relation of volume of production to volume of exports, as well as a commitment to Mexicanize within a certain period of time in the future.

The industrial plan may run into some difficulties with products exported to the United States that have been produced under a system of fiscal and other incentives. These products may have to pay countervailing duties when entering the U.S. market. There is a mechanism within GATT, however, that allows incentives if they are necessary for economic development of an LDC. Other areas of concern to foreign investors are the financial self-determination and export programs. In the case of the automobile industry, the decree that determines the behavior of an already established, 100 percent foreign-owned automobile industry requires the auto industry to export progressively more products to earn sufficient foreign exchange to compensate for their imports. At the same time, it requires increased Mexican integration of the finished vehicle. A limiting factor is price control on trucks. This automotive decree is interesting because it shows the industrial development plan and the foreign investment law in actual operation.

U.S. multinationals, in order to operate in Mexico under the industrial development plan, will have to share their export markets with their Mexican affiliates in accord with negotiations in each sector. The latest sector to be accommodated within the plan is the pharmaceutical industry. Recent government agreement calls for reduction of foreign equity from 85 to 49 percent and limits imports of raw materials to 57 percent of the total value. It also establishes a Mexican center for pharmaceutical investigation to determine how to increase exports at least 20 percent per annum.

For the foreseeable future all industrial investment will follow the development plan. Most investments will be in the priority of Categories number I and II. Category I includes investment in agro-industry and capital goods; Category II includes investments in nondurable consumer goods, durable consumer goods, and intermediate goods. The priority regional areas are:

Zone I

This includes the industrial ports of Coatzacoalcos, Tampico, Salina Cruz, and Lazaro Cárdenas, and the principal border localities and the corridor that joins the cities of Queretaro, Queretaro, and León, Guanajuato. Most of these areas are located on or near the natural gas distribution network, and they have water, labor supply, adequate communications, and infrastructure. In the case of the industrial ports, the aim is to manufacture for export, as well as to export goods from other areas.

Zone II

This category is made up of state priority zones, which state governments may select for the location of industrial activities best suited for their respective states. State industrial parks should fall into this category.

Zone III

This zone covers areas subject to control and regulation. These are the already congested areas, such as the valley of Mexico, Guadalajara, and Monterrey. For practical purposes, these are no-growth zones.

Under the industrial plan the benefits to a firm will depend on what it will manufacture and where it will locate. A business manufacturing Category I products and located in Zone I is in a position to receive maximum benefits.

The first annual results (1979–80) of the National Industrial Development Plan show a total of $8.3 billion committed in new industrial investment programs, creating almost 113,000 jobs. This investment will be made in Priority 1 and 2 industrial categories. Of the new products reported, 52 percent are new plants, and the remaining 48 percent are expansions of existing industrial facilities. The majority of the total investment committed, 71.4 percent, is in agroindustry and capital goods. The vast majority of dollar volume (approximately $3.2 billion) is destined for capital goods, $2.6 billion for strategic industrial inputs, and only $156 million in agroindustry projects. In this first report there were no indications about the percentages of private and public sector investment, nor about national against foreign origin.

Law to Promote Mexican Investment and Regulate Foreign Investment

The law to promote Mexican investment and regulate foreign investment, approved by the Mexican Congress in 1973, is probably the most important Mexican legislation since the presidential decrees of 1942, 1944, and 1945 established that any foreign company or Mexican company that acquires foreign partners would require a prior permit from the secretary of foreign relations. One of the prerequisites of such a permit was to subscribe to a doctrine known in all of Latin America and the United States as the "Calvo Clause." This was elaborated by an Argentinian, Carlos Calvo, during the second half of the nineteenth century. It states that a foreigner must consider himself as a national of (in this case) Mexico, must submit to the Mexican courts, and must not seek special protection from his government. This doctrine permeates all Mexican legislation related to foreign investment.

From this point until the foreign investment law of 1973 became effective, there was a series of decrees, laws, and administrative decisions that affected foreign investment, to the degree that the major complaint from foreign investors was that the Mexican government was constantly changing the rules in the middle of the game. Meanwhile, the Mexican private sector and the legal community sought a comprehensive law to regulate foreign investment. The law finally adopted, like many other Mexican laws, was written in such a way as to allow for pragmatic flexibility in order to accommodate current situations as they arose.

When the law first became known, the foreign investment community felt that it was harsher than expected. Combined with the laws on the transfer of technology and patents and trademarks, it caused foreign investors to shy away from investing in Mexico. It was obvious that Mexico needed and wanted foreign investment, but on its own terms. The early interpretation of the law was quite inflexible and seemed to be antibusiness and anti–U.S. Statistics in those years showed that foreign investment will not flow to a country where it is not wanted. The foreign investment law is aimed, on the one hand, at stimulating Mexican national investment and, on the other, at specifying the conditions under which foreign investment may enter Mexico. It is difficult to find anything in this law that stimulates Mexican investment, other than the general philosophy that foreign investment is welcome when it complements national investment and does not displace existing business enterprise.

The law brings together all the different dispositions previously established to control foreign investment. In this sense it satisfies the alleged need for a single law on the subject. It spells out which activities are reserved exclusively for the state, such as petroleum (nationalized in 1938) and other hydrocarbons, basic petrochemicals, exploitation of radioactive minerals, electricity (nationalized in 1960), railroads, and communications. Reserved for Mexican citizens or Mexican companies, to the exclusion of foreigners, are activities such as radio and television and air and maritime transport. Foreign investment can participate with an equity of anywhere from 30 to 40 percent, depending on the activity and geographical area. The National Commission on Foreign Investment can make exceptions when it considers it convenient for the country's economy.

The commission was created by the foreign investment law and given broad powers to administer the law. It was originally composed of seven secretaries: secretary of interior (gobernación), foreign relations, treasury, national patrimony, commerce, labor, and the Presidency. The commission is required to meet once a month, and the sessions are chaired in rotating order. Although the secretaries are charged with the responsibility of the commission, this responsibility can be delegated to undersecretaries, who act as alternates.

An executive secretary is appointed by the President to assist the commission. As the commission sees fit, it can delegate responsibility and authority to the executive secretary to resolve matters of routine nature or where a precedent has been established. The commission also has a technical commission to screen proposed foreign investment projects and make recommendations to the full commission. The executive secretary is also available for informal discussions on a proposed investment. These are very helpful to the investor as they allow for greater understanding and orientation prior to the submission of a formal application.

The commission either approves or rejects projects by foreigners to invest in Mexico. Once the committee does approve a project, then all secretaries of the Mexican government are informed and assigned their responsibilities. This is a very important coordinating step, now inherent in the commission approval. For example, prior to the foreign investment law and the commission, permission for investments was granted by both the secretaries of industry and commerce and of foreign relations. It was often the case that projects required the installation of new roads, electrical substations, telephone lines, or water wells, and the secretaries responsible for each of the complementary installations were not aware of their responsibilities. This created bureaucratic obstacles and unnecessary delays.

Under Mexican law, no foreigners may own land in areas one hundred kilometers wide along the Mexican border and fifty kilometers wide inland from the coast. The foreign investment law, however, allows Mexican credit institutions to act in trust for thirty years, so that foreigners may invest in these areas. This pertains largely to the tourist zones. In the case of "in-bond" plants, or *maquiladoras*, the factory and office facilities are leased.

The foreign investment law very carefully monitors and regulates the acquisition of stock and capital or fixed assets in existing Mexican companies by a foreigner or a foreign corporation. Prior to the foreign investment law, some foreign investment entered Mexico by the acquisition of an already existing company. In some cases, these acquisitions were handled very quietly and without public notice; in others, public outcry caused the government to become very vigilant in this area.

The National Registry of Foreign Investment, also created under the law, now operates under the auspices of the undersecretary of industrial development and national patrimony. All foreigners or foreign-controlled corporations that undertake investment in Mexico are registered with the National Registry of Foreign Investment.

We have discussed the foreign investment law and have seen how it regulates two very important aspects of foreign investment. One is equity participation, and the other is management. Nothing has been said about regulating management which, according to the law, may not exceed capital participation. The third and last element to control adequately foreign investment is the law on transfer of technology and the use and exploitation of patents and trademarks.

The Law on Transfer of Technology and the Use of Patents and Trademarks

The objective of the law on the transfer of technology and the use and exploitation of patents and trademarks is to help the Mexican entrepreneur obtain the best technology under the most favorable market conditions. The purpose of the law is

> to eliminate obstacles to Mexico's development and foreign trade, to adjust technology contracts to the guidelines of the government's industrialization policy, and to stimulate the creation of a local scientific and technological infrastructure that permits the adaptation of foreign technology to the conditions and needs of the Mexican economy.

Like the foreign investment law, the technology law requires registry of all contracts for the transfer of technology. This provides a record of the terms of the contract under which technology is being sold to a Mexican company. A contract is not approved if it is found that it does not comply with the many requisites established in the law. Technology contracts were being negotiated based on 3 to 5 percent of sales. Obviously there were some exceptions.

Under present-day conditions, and in order to implement the industrial development plan, the present philosophy of the secretariat of national patrimony is that Mexico has practically exhausted the purchase of technology at the rate of 3 to 5 percent on sales. All other technology was being withheld, and now the Mexican government recognizes that it must pay a higher and more competitive price for the technology it requires.

The law of invention and trademarks

> regulates the granting of patents of invention, the registration of industrial models and designs, the registration of trademarks, denomination of origin, and trade names and advertisements, as well as the repression of unfair competition in relation to the rights granted in this law.

This law is relevant to foreign investment by limiting the degree to which a U.S. multinational corporation would risk its patents, trademarks, and other trade secrets. The law thereby limits economic activity within the country. For example, a U.S. multinational would not submit a new process patented in the United States to its Mexican affiliate in a 49 to 51 percent equity position unless it was absolutely sure the patent registered in Mexico would be protected.

Another example is the requisite of the patent and trademark law that all trademarks of foreign origin must be used in conjunction with a mark originally registered in Mexico. This aspect of the law gave such concern to the foreign investment community that some multinational corporations were threatening to withdraw their investments. Fortunately, most of the harsh measures of this law are being reconsidered.

One distinct and unique advantage of multinational corporations is their ability to hasten economic development by bringing to the host country the latest technology. A host country that places in jeopardy the patents, trademarks, and technology of multinational corporations is denying itself a valuable contribution to economic development.

Investment—Conclusion

U.S. direct private foreign investment in Mexico continues to decline as a percentage of total. At the beginning of the last decade, the U.S. share of total foreign investment was approximately 81 percent; ten years later it had declined to approximately 70 percent, losing ground to West Germany, England, Japan, and others. Almost 80 percent of U.S. investment in Mexico is largely in industry, with commerce, banking, and service absorbing the balance.

The future of U.S. direct private investment in Mexico is bright. The rules for entering Mexico are quite clear, although not altogether acceptable to some multinationals. The rapid expansion of Mexico's economy; the need to manufacture capital goods; the requirements of the domestic market for consumer goods; the availability of petrochemical feedstock; the availability of energy, not only crude and gas, but also hydroelectric and thermoelectric; and the availability of a large labor force all point to unique opportunities for foreign investors.

The ratio of 51 percent Mexican capital to 49 percent foreign capital is too limiting for Mexico's economic development. At the present time, lack of availability of Mexican partners with 51 percent of the capital for investment in a joint venture presents a serious bottleneck.

Although the National Industrial Development Plan allows for Mexicanization at a future date, it is better to Mexicanize, if possible, at the onset when risk capital is required and Mexican partners can be more useful. Mexicanization is the process whereby any foreign investment, unless otherwise exempt, is required to sell 51 percent of its equity to Mexican nationals. This can be accomplished in several ways. One way is to find Mexican partners; another is to place the stock in escrow until suitable partners are found; and another way is through the Mexican Stock Exchange.

Recent Mexicanizations have taken place through the stock market, but the Foreign Investment Commission has not approved of further Mexicanization by this process because it feels this does not really Mexicanize the operation, since the 49 percent held by the foreign company controls the operations (the 51 percent owned by Mexicans being dispersed as stock shares). The commission recognizes the stock market as a source of capital formation, however, and is searching for an equitable formula for Mexicanization through the stock market.

The foreign investment law, the transfer of technology law, the law that controls patents and trademarks, and other measures (including administrative decrees) are designed to control foreign investment. When one speaks of foreign investment in Mexico, the reference is to the U.S. direct private foreign investment. The same mistrust toward U.S. trade policies exists toward U.S. investment in Mexico, the notion being that U.S. investment is an extension of U.S. policy to make Mexico dependent.

The investment climate in Mexico has always been characterized by a great deal of rhetoric, some of which became translated into actual deeds, such as the legislation to regulate foreign investment. The rhetoric often presages changes in foreign investment. Most of it is a result of fears, justified or not, of the presence of U.S. multinationals in Mexico; political manipulations to make U.S. multinationals the "whipping boys"; or ideological arguments by those who would like to see free enterprise, private initiative, and U.S. business presence disappear from the Mexican economic scene.

One fear that has been expressed is that U.S. multinationals are too big and powerful and are tools of the United States government [*sic*]. Their tremendous economic and political resources create unfair competition and unreal pricing and exercise undue influence on host governments. However, serious investigation easily disproves these allegations. For most U.S. multinationals, being a "whipping boy" is not unusual, especially where economic woes beset an administration of a Third World country. They are accused of causing inflation, high prices, devaluation of currencies, etc. Rhetoric in the communications media, television, radio, and newspapers, turns into diatribe. It takes a great deal of equanimity on the part of U.S. multinationals to withstand such an onslaught. This type of demagoguery poisons the investment climate not only for foreign investment, but also for local national investment as well, by creating a generally hostile attitude toward business.

Ideological reasons such as the following underlie much of the criticism of U.S. multinationals.

1. They decapitalize the country,
2. promote consumerism,
3. exploit workers,
4. make exorbitant profits,
5. are monopolistic, and
6. corrupt government officials.

It is not the purpose of this chapter to judge the validity of the allegations made against U.S. multinationals in Mexico, but it is necessary to explain from time to time that investments from capital-exporting countries, such as the United States, will not enter a country if it is felt that foreign investment is not wanted to the extent that profits are prejudiced. Political and monetary stability in Mexico are usually two of the main incentives for investing there. A growing domestic market and absence of foreign exchange controls continue to be attractions in Mexico.

U.S. multinationals in any host country must consider how their presence affects the environment in which they operate. Certainly, producing a product, paying taxes, creating jobs, and efficient management are their prime responsibility, whether they operate in the United States or in Mexico. When operating in foreign countries, however, a new dimension is added to the cliché "the role of business is business." This is the assumption of corporate responsibilities toward the community, state, and nation. Some companies refer to "paying their social rent." A U.S. multinational that is aware of the host nation's national goals and aspirations and makes a positive contribution toward these goals will be regarded as a good corporate citizen.

The National Industrial Development Plan of Mexico clearly spells out national goals. Every foreign investor should be familiar not only with these goals, but with the aspirations of the Mexican people to education, self-sufficiency in agriculture, eradication of disease, and an opportunity for U.S. multinationals to become engaged in programs that, in one degree or another, signify an awareness of their social responsibility.

Wayne A. Cornelius

5

Immigration, Mexican Development Policy, and the Future of U.S.-Mexican Relations

Introduction

One of the rationales frequently advanced for restricting Mexican immigration into the United States holds that only by adopting drastic measures to reduce the flow of migrants can the U.S. compel the kinds of public policy changes in Mexico that would be needed to cut the migration off at its source. The argument usually begins by noting the failure of a series of Mexican governments to manage the nation's economic development so as to create enough jobs for willing citizens, and the failure until very recently to mount a serious population control effort. Massive unemployment and underemployment in Mexico are attributed to a preference on the part of public and private sector elites for capital-intensive development producing little employment. And the United States has enabled Mexican elites to pursue this kind of development by keeping open the safety valve of emigration.

According to this view, heavy migration to the U.S.—whether tem-

---

WAYNE A. CORNELIUS *is director of the Program in United States–Mexican Studies at the University of California, San Diego. Dr. Cornelius is a well-known author specializing in the area of immigration.*

porary or permanent in character—does not really contribute to development in economically depressed source regions. Its main effect is to preserve, or even intensify, existing structures of economic exploitation, a highly unequal distribution of wealth, and the positions and privileges of Mexican politicians and local *caciques* ("bosses"). The human escape hatch thus helps buy time for a corrupt oligarchy, allowing Mexican elites to export dissension and thereby avert popular pressures for overdue reforms. By allowing the border to remain porous, the U.S. not only condones a morally unacceptable status quo in Mexico, but also may actually increase the likelihood of a violent social revolution in Mexico, the outcome of which could be highly detrimental to U.S. interests.

All this suggests that the U.S. must act boldly to put Mexican elites on notice that we will no longer tolerate high levels of illegal immigration, and that they will have to face up to their own problems of poverty, overpopulation, and unemployment. "Bold action," in this context, usually involves greatly augmented enforcement activity by the U.S. Border Patrol and legislation penalizing U.S. employers who knowingly hire illegal migrants. The time frame for immigration restriction varies among proponents of this approach. Some advocate an abrupt tight seal of the U.S.–Mexico border (no matter what manpower and other resources are necessary to achieve that); others argue that new restrictive measures should be phased in gradually, over a period of, say, five years, in order to give Mexico time to wean itself from reliance on the U.S. labor market. These "gradualists" would also offer compensatory measures to cushion the impact of a cutoff of employment opportunities in the U.S., such as a "transitional" (time-delimited and declining) guest worker program, trade concessions, and economic development assistance.

Whatever the variations on implementation, the rationale for all these proposals is identical: the shock therapy provided by a major escalation of U.S. border enforcement efforts and vigorous enforcement of employer sanctions legislation is needed to elicit appropriate policy responses from Mexico. The "appropriate" responses, in this view, would amount to nothing less than a fundamental reorientation of Mexico's development strategy, as practiced during the past forty years, toward a principal emphasis on employment creation (even at the expense of higher rates of aggregate economic growth), income redistribution, and investment of the bulk of government earnings from oil and gas exports in small-scale rural development projects. Only when Mexican decision makers are put under severe pressure by the U.S., it is believed, will they pursue development policies that directly promote employment creation and income equality. Only in this way can the U.S. make sure that enough of Mexico's hydrocarbon wealth will be invested in ways that will significantly diminish the "push" factors which drive Mexican workers into U.S. labor markets. Otherwise, Mexican elites have no interest—objective or perceived—in taking steps to diminish emigration.

Some radical critics of the present Mexican system have embraced this "bludgeon" approach to reducing illegal migration from Mexico as a way of "deepening the contradictions," a way of hastening the outbreak of social upheavals and the ultimate destruction of an unjust socioeconomic order and the political system that supports it. Presumably, withdrawing the U.S. "subsidy" to Mexican elites—free use of the U.S. labor market as a dumping ground for surplus workers—would improve prospects for replacing the existing regime with a more equity-oriented government.

Other proponents, more concerned with maintaining political stability in Mexico than with fomenting a revolutionary upheaval, argue that U.S. action to cut off illegal migration would actually *assist* the Mexican political regime in convincing Mexican economic elites that their self-interest depends upon making fundamental changes in Mexico's economic and social structures and reducing the country's "increasingly needless" economic dependence on the United States. Thus, it is argued, cutting off the flow of migrants to the U.S. would serve to prop up the existing system rather than undermine it, while raising living standards for the Mexican poor.

Those taking this position point out that the resource constraints which may have prevented previous Mexican administrations from doing more to combat poverty and unemployment have been lifted. Recent oil and gas discoveries in Mexico (proven reserves of 60 billion barrels, as of September 1980) are cited as evidence that Mexico now has all the resources it needs to provide jobs for all its citizens, eliminate poverty, raise living standards, even out the distribution of wealth, and curb population growth. Now more than ever, Mexico's elites are "undeserving" of their "foreign aid" from the United States.

Proponents of this argument tend to place most or all of the blame for illegal immigration upon Mexico, citing particularly its failure (until lately) to control population growth and its failure to invest public resources in ways that would increase employment. They conveniently neglect the past and continuing role of the United States in fomenting labor migration from Mexico. A migration flow that was initiated by U.S. labor recruiters operating in Mexico in the 1880s, sustained by high U.S. employer demand ever since, and officially welcomed by the U.S. government during seventy-seven out of the last one hundred years is now attributed to "push factors" in Mexico caused by the developmental failures of Mexican elites. Mexican elites are castigated for the preference for capital-intensive, labor-displacing investments, while the employment implications of U.S. private investments in Mexico—which tend to be *more* capital-intensive than Mexican domestic investments—are ignored.

To those who prefer to blame the contemporary immigration problem on "irresponsible" Mexican decision makers, the history of U.S. involvements in Mexican development is irrelevant, or simply inconvenient. Their basic position is that "the U.S. doesn't owe Mexico anything," and certainly nothing to the Mexican political elite. The tendency is to see Mexico as a spoiled child—a petulant, ungrateful one, at that!—who has already gotten away with too much and must be "disciplined" by tough U.S. law enforcement efforts if it is ever to mend its ways.

This perspective on the Mexican immigration phenomenon raises some fundamental questions about the willingness and the capacity of the Mexican regime to come to grips with the country's developmental problems. Specifically, it assumes that:

1. the Mexican government has ample capacity to produce a short-term (not just a long-term) solution to the country's employment problem;
2. Mexican officials choose not to exercise this capacity because the U.S., in its generosity, keeps open the human safety valve of emigration;
3. Mexico's oil wealth can be translated readily into jobs and higher living standards for poor people in those parts of the country that supply most of the migrants to the U.S.; and
4. Mexican elites have no objective interest in pursuing policies that would reduce emigration and, unless put under pressure by U.S. actions, will continue to callously ignore the basic human needs of their population.

All these assumptions merit much closer scrutiny than they customarily receive in the U.S. debate over immigration policy. How valid are these assumptions empirically? Do they constitute an appropriate, realistic basis for U.S. decisions on immigration policy? How would Mexican elites respond to a more punitive stance by the U.S. on illegal immigration? These are the questions to which this chapter is addressed. We begin by examining the magnitude of the unemployment/underemployment problem in Mexico today and the prospects for solving it, *regardless* of the priority attached to the problem by Mexican officials in the next two decades.

Dimensions of the Problem

There are no official, national-level statistics on unemployment in Mexico, but one estimate prepared under the auspices of the Mexican Ministry of Labor set open unemployment in 1978 at 6.9 percent, and underemployment at 50.3 percent. Independent estimates by the Economic Commission for Latin America (ECLA) found open unemployment in Mexican cities to be about 7 percent in 1978 and 6 percent in 1979. But economists estimate that about two-thirds of all unemployed or underemployed workers in Mexico are in the agricultural sector. A 1979 study by the Banco Nacional de Crédito Rural (BAN-RURAL) found that out of 7,252,000 working-age rural dwellers, over 5 million were unemployed or underemployed—a rate of nearly 70 percent. If that rate still holds, there are more than 5.7 million underemployed or unemployed working-age Mexicans in rural areas alone (based on 1980 precensus estimates of the rural labor force). Nationally, the "backlog" of underemployed and unemployed workers is probably about 10 million, and at least 700,000 *new* job seekers enter the Mexican labor market each year. In addition, there is probably a rotating pool of 1 to 3 million working-age Mexicans who work at least part of each year in the United States (including "permanent legal resident aliens," who are still based primarily in Mexico, and undocumented migrants). Thus the total number of jobs that would have to be created in Mexico during the next twenty years in order to (a) accommodate all new entrants to the labor force, (b) absorb the present arrears of unemployed and underemployed into productive full-time employment, and (c) reintegrate those who would otherwise be employed in the United States is *31 to 33 million jobs.*

It should be kept in mind that massive expansion of employment opportunities would have to occur during a period in which the demand for labor in all sectors of the Mexican economy is declining, and particularly in agriculture. Agricultural mechanization continues to displace large numbers of workers each year, and, throughout the economy, relatively cheap (government subsidized) energy encourages the substitution of capital for labor. To the extent that the government's rural development programs succeed in making agricultural land more productive (therefore more valuable), more small holdings will be absorbed (through rental or purchase) into large-scale commercial farms whose labor requirements are typically less.

Despite heavy out-migration during the past four decades, about 25 to 26 million Mexicans still live in rural areas (about 40 percent of the national population), and their numbers are expected to increase to 35 to 37 million by the year 2000. Thus by the end of the century, between 8.3 and 10.5 million working-age Mexicans will still need to find employment in the agricultural sector. During the 1980s at least, some 300,000 new job seekers will enter the agricultural labor force each year. Of course, growing numbers of these rural workers will seek and find employment in urban services and manufacturing. But others will go to the United States. A nationwide survey of 62,500 Mexican households conducted in late 1978 and early 1979 found that nearly 80 percent of Mexican migrants to the United States still originate in rural areas (defined as localities of fewer than 20,000 inhabitants). Thus if there is to be a sharp reduction in the flow of U.S.–bound migrants, very large numbers of new jobs must be created in the rural sector. And most experts doubt the feasibility of increasing the labor-absorptive capacity of Mexican agriculture by that magnitude, even with the most successful efforts to bring new land into cultivation, expand irrigation, and build new labor-intensive food-processing plants in close proximity to peasant communities.

The key factor that will affect the magnitude of the unemployment/ underemployment problem in Mexico during the remainder of this century is the entry into an already tight job market of millions of young workers born in the 1950s and 1960s. This guarantees that the Mexican labor force will grow by at least 3.4 percent annually, at least through 1990. Due to rapidly falling fertility rates since the late 1960s, Mexico's rate of *total* population growth is now below 2.9 percent per year. This rate will continue to decline, in response to rising educational levels, continued urbanization of the population, and the Mexican government's family planning program. But the decline in the total fertility rate will not begin to show up in the form of lower *labor force* growth rate until sometime in the late 1980s. And the smaller numbers of children (future labor force entrants) being born in the 1970s and 1980s will be offset to some extent by the larger numbers of adult women who are expected to seek employment outside the home during the next two decades. Mexico is, therefore, demographically locked into a huge expansion of its working-age, economically active population during the remainder of this century, *regardless* of current or future successes in promoting birth control.

Economic Growth and Job Creation: Possibilities for 1980–2000

Most economists now estimate that if Mexico's current petroleum-based economic boom can be maintained through the remainder of this century, with no drastic changes in the structure of the economy or the basic model of development, the Mexican economy will just barely be able to absorb the anticipated new entrants to the labor force during this period, but there will be no appreciable reduction in the "backlog" of underemployed and unemployed workers.

Projections by Clark W. Reynolds of Stanford University show that a minimum, sustained (not just average) economic growth rate (in GNP terms) of 6.6 percent per annum would be necessary to generate enough jobs to accommodate the 20 million new entrants to the labor force in 1980–2000. But that rate of growth would not be sufficient to cut into the arrears of unemployment/underemployment. To absorb the arrears of about 10 million workers, the GNP would have to grow at a sustained rate of well over 7 percent each year until the end of the century. That would be a record of sustained economic growth that is virtually unprecedented among developing countries.

Moreover, the capital investment requirements for wiping out the backlog of unemployment/underemployment are staggering. Current costs of creating permanent jobs in the Mexican economy range from over $30,000 per job in the agricultural sector to more than $250,000 per job (in 1980 dollars) in the petrochemical industry. At an incremental investment cost of $30,000 per job, an annual investment of $21 billion would be needed just to absorb the new entrants to the labor force. Even if, through use of more labor-intensive technologies and other means, the capital outlay for each job created could be reduced to $10,000, $7 billion would have to be invested in job-creating projects each year in order to accommodate the annual increment to the labor force. To fully absorb the present backlog of underemployed or unemployed workers over a five-year period, at $10,000 per new permanent job created, would require an *additional* investment of $20 billion each year, or $10 billion per year if the labor-absorption process were spread out over ten years. Thus in order to both accommodate the new entrants to the labor force *and* eliminate the current backlog, there would have to be total job-creating investments of $27 billion per year (if the backlog were to be absorbed within five years), or $17 billion per year (if elimination of the arrears is spread out over ten years), *assuming an incremental investment cost of only $10,000 per job.*

How feasible and realistic is this level of job-creating investment in a country where gross capital investment (by both public and private sectors) totalled $29.8 billion in 1979, of which a much smaller amount is actually related to permanent job creation? Public sector investments are more job-creating than private sector investments, and the former constitute only 46 percent of total capital investment. Moreover, the bulk of public sector investment is in infrastructure (dams, highways, electrical transmission lines, oil and gas pipelines), housing, factory buildings, and other physical structures which employ considerable temporary labor in their construction but which, once built, require few permanent workers.

How do Mexico's oil and gas earnings stack up against these investment requirements? In 1980, total earnings from oil and gas exports were expected to be $14 billion, of which only about $7 billion would be available for investment in potentially job-creating projects. As shown in Figure 1, nearly one-third of the export earnings during the 1980–82 period will be reabsorbed by PEMEX, the Mexican government oil and gas monopoly, for exploration, construction of new production and refining facilities, pipelines, and so forth. Of the remaining two-thirds ($9.3 billion in 1980), 24 percent will be consumed by social expenditures (education, health care, etc.). That leaves about half ($7.1 billion in 1980) of total oil and gas revenues for investment in job-creating projects in agriculture and rural development, communications and transportation, industry (other than PEMEX), and public works to be built by state and local governments. Even if only 25 percent of the revenues are reinvested in the oil sector, that would free up only about $1 billion more annually for job-creating investments.

Fig. 1.   Allocation of oil resources 1980–1982

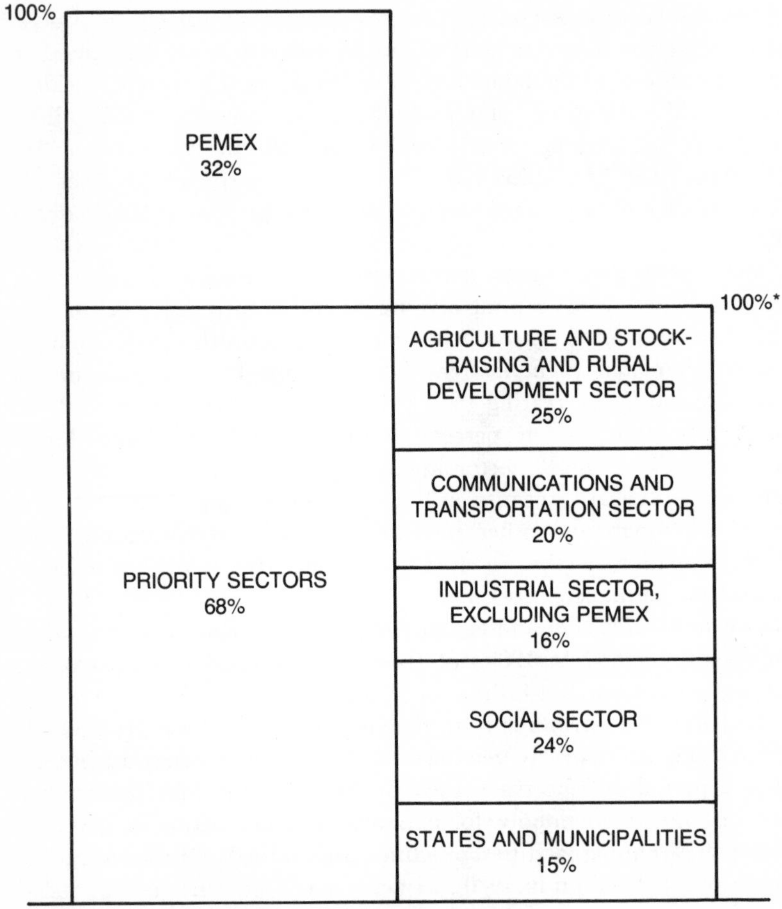

*Excluding the resources to be absorbed by PEMEX

Source: United Mexican States, Ministry of Programing and Budget, *The Global Development Plan, 1980–1981: Synopsis,* 1980, p. 35.

The Lopez Portillo administration has set some ambitious goals for employment creation (see Table 1). The Global Development Plan for 1980–82 envisions the creation of more than 2.2 million jobs (averaging 730,000 per year). That would represent a 4.2 percent per year

TABLE 1. EMPLOYMENT CREATION IN MEXICO, 1979–1982
(THOUSANDS OF PERSONS TO BE EMPLOYED)

Year	Total	New Entrants to Labor Force	Arrears of Unemployed/ Underemployed
1979	660.0 *	(not available)	(not available)
1980	695.1	683.1	12.0
1981	731.1	717.1	13.9
1982	814.7	779.5	35.2
1980–1982 Total	2,240.9	2,179.7	61.1

* Actual number of new jobs created in 1979, according to Mexican Finance Minister David Ibarra, as reported in Cecil Scaglione, "Mexico Looks to the Future," *The San Diego Union*, April 26, 1980.

Source: Comisión Consultativa del Empleo, Secretaría del Trabajo y Previsión Social, *Programa Nacional de Empleo 1980/82 (Proyecto): Presentación resumida,* December 1979, Anexo Gráfico, p. 6.

growth rate in employment, which would bring open unemployment down to 5.5 percent and underemployment down to 40.8 percent by the end of 1982, according to government estimates. In 1979, only about 660,000 new jobs were reportedly created. Even if jobs are created at a rate of more than 800,000 per year, that rate of employment growth would still be adequate only to absorb the annual increment to the national labor force and make a tiny dent in the backlog of unemployed or underemployed persons. And if the arrears are absorbed at the rate of only 35,000 per year (the government's target for 1982, as shown in Table 1), it would take 286 years to wipe out the existing backlog of about 10 million unemployed and underemployed persons!

In assessing the impact of the employment creation on migration to the United States, it must be kept in mind that most of the new

jobs to be created are in urban industry, construction, and services—
not in the rural sector where the vast majority of migrants to the U.S.
still originate. The government's target for growth in agricultural
employment is much more modest: only about 247,000 jobs per year
over the 1980–82 period. An independent estimate of the job-creating
potential of Mexican federal public investments in agriculture and
rural development during the same period is even lower (an average
of 177,581 new permanent jobs per year), although a large increase
in *temporary* jobs is projected for the rural sector. It is clear, however,
that the rate of permanent employment growth envisioned by the
government is not even sufficient to keep pace with the additions to
the rural labor force (about 300,000 new job seekers each year), let
alone to reduce the backlog of rural unemployed/underemployed
workers.

This illustrates a more general difficulty with using highly aggre-
gated employment growth targets and projections. In the aggregate,
such targets may be realistic and attainable. But we cannot expect *all*
segments of the Mexican labor market to grow at an equal rate. Jobs
for urban-based, skilled workers will grow far more rapidly than jobs
for unskilled agricultural laborers. So even after two decades of extremely high overall growth rates, there will still be a surplus of low-
skilled workers—particularly in rural areas and small cities—while
significant shortages of certain types of skilled workers will have developed. Indeed, some of those shortages (e.g., skilled construction
workers) are already apparent in the larger cities. Rapid growth—even
at 1979–80 rates of 8 or 9 percent per year—cannot and will not correct the structural imbalances in the Mexican economy. It is precisely
those structural imbalances that generated a backlog of 10 million
unemployed and underemployed workers, despite aggregate GNP
growth averaging more than 6 percent per annum during the 1950
to 1975 period.

In short, it is difficult to escape the conclusion that there will continue to be a significant labor surplus in Mexico, particularly in those
local labor markets that now supply most migrants to the U.S., well
into the next century, *regardless* of what development plan is followed
by the Mexican government and *regardless* of what pressures are applied by the United States to promote more labor-intensive development in Mexico.

Reducing the "Push Factors": Obstacles and Constraints

Even with optimal kinds and levels of employment-generating investments by the public sector in Mexico, there are numerous obstacles and offsetting forces that are likely to complicate the task of reducing unemployment and other "push factors" inducing emigration. For example, the rate of female labor force participation in Mexico is still relatively low by U.S. standards, but declining fertility (less childbearing) will increase female labor force participation. So Mexican women will contribute more than their traditional share to the expansion of the labor force. Thus, even though the long-term impact of declining fertility will be to ameliorate the unemployment problem, its short-term effect will be to exacerbate the problem.

To the extent that rural development projects are successful in creating jobs (for example, in food-processing industry), they will induce more women to enter the labor force, just as the border area manufacturing assembly plants (*maquiladoras*) have done. Surveys have found that 72 to 78 percent of the workers employed in these plants are young, single women, most of whom were born and raised in the borderlands and many of whom would not otherwise be employed outside the home.

Rapid inflation—20 percent in 1979 and at least 30 percent in 1980 —will continue to erode real incomes, especially among the poor who are not unionized and do not even receive the official minimum wage (which includes nearly 48 percent of the country's work force). Real wages have declined each year since 1977, and this trend may persist as the massive influx of *petropesos* and sharp increases in all kinds of government spending continue to overheat the Mexican economy. But high levels of government spending will be needed to maintain economic growth rates of 8 percent or more per year, and without those high growth rates it will clearly be impossible to attain government targets for job creation. With inflation in Mexico running at a rate two to two-and-a-half times that of the United States, the real wage differential is already more than 7:1 for most low-skilled jobs in the southwestern United States compared with Mexico generally. The real wage differential in manufacturing ranges between 3:1 and 6:1; for agriculture and many low-skilled service occupations, it seems

116Wayne A. Cornelius

to range between 8:1 and 13:1. These differentials would widen even more if the Mexican peso were devalued again, as it was in 1976. In any event, one of the most potent incentives for migrating to the U.S.—the very large real wage differential—is likely to become even more powerful in the foreseeable future. Rapid inflation will hit the lowest income population hardest and will increase their need to supplement their cash income even to purchase food and other basic necessities.

Mexico's oil industry itself will never absorb, directly, more than a tiny fraction of the country's surplus workers. PEMEX is Mexico's single largest employer, with a work force of about 100,000, which may expand to about 150,000 workers in the next few years. But most of this additional employment will be temporary in nature (primarily construction jobs), and, relative to the rest of the economy, the highly capital-intensive oil and petrochemical industries will yield few permanent jobs.

As Mexico's oil boom develops, the massive influx of public and private investment capital into the hydrocarbons sector may have a *negative* impact on total job creation, by diverting capital ("bidding it away") from some of the more labor-intensive sectors of the economy. Thus, the huge investments needed to develop the oil-petrochemical sector may be detrimental to employment to the extent that they are financed with capital that would have found other, probably more labor-intensive, uses.

Even in the agricultural sector, "successful" rural development projects may end up pushing more people out of agriculture than are absorbed or retained. To the extent that such projects promote further mechanization and concentration of landholdings, they will be directly labor-displacing. They will also raise aspirations for economic mobility, reduce isolation, facilitate long-distance travel, and increase rural family incomes to the point where peasants are able to finance the cost of migration, at least for some members of the household. Too much poverty seems to paralyze potential migrants; the alleviation of rural poverty increases peasant mobility. It is no accident that most migration to the U.S. stems from Mexico's "middle-developed" states, not the most impoverished ones like Guerrero, Oaxaca, Chiapas, and the Yucatán.

Mexico's unemployment and underemployment problems cannot be solved simply by throwing more money at them. The Mexican government, the World Bank, the Inter-American Development Bank, and a host of other development institutions are already spending billions of dollars each year on potentially job-creating projects, most of them located in the countryside. During the 1980–82 period, the Mexican government alone will spend an average of $2.3 billion per year on rural development projects (an average public investment of $1,150 for each of the country's poor rural families). This will constitute about 25 percent of total federal investment, excluding the oil sector, up from 15 percent in the mid-1970s. By prevailing international standards, this is a high level of public investment in rural development.

Even higher levels may be needed (e.g., 40 to 45 percent, comparable to the 44 percent of public revenues that were invested in rural development during the 1935 to 1945 period) during the 1980s in order to have a significant impact on rural unemployment and underemployment. It is doubtful, however, that the Mexican government possesses the administrative, technical, and political capacity to mount the massive, directly job-creating programs that would be necessary to provide permanent employment for more than 65 to 70 percent of the country's work force during the next twenty years. To accomplish more in the short term would involve not just pumping far larger amounts of public resources into high unemployment/poverty areas, but overcoming major, longstanding problems of inefficient resource mobilization, corruption, mismanagement, and insensitivity to the needs and preferences of people in the areas to be benefited.

Any abrupt shift toward a much more labor-intensive strategy of development is likely to arouse serious political resistance from vested interests, both domestic and foreign. At the local and state levels, there are still numerous *caciques* ("political bosses") who are in a position to effectively block implementation of federal government programs that threaten their personal economic interests. At the national level, highly conservative business, industrial, and financial elites who still exert enormous influence over capital formation and investment in the Mexican economy are likely to view such a shift with considerable suspicion if not open hostility. It must be kept in mind that the needed jobs must be created in the context of a mixed, market economy—not a socialist, "command" economy—in which the private sector still controls more than half of all investment capital and has the capacity to instigate large-scale capital flight (as it did in the last year of Luís Echeverría's Presidency). For example, two privately owned banking groups, BANCOMER and BANAMEX, rank well ahead of the majority of state-controlled banks in total assets and investable resources. U.S. bankers, to whom Mexico owes more than $12 billion, might also tend to view a drastic shift toward labor-intensive development as promoting "make-work" projects that squander scarce savings needed for more productive investments.

The kind of economic development needed to significantly reduce low-end poverty, unemployment, and income inequality in Mexico may not be possible *in the absence of* fundamental structural changes in the Mexican economy and political system. Such sweeping changes may, indeed, be a necessary precondition for the effective use of oil revenues to create large numbers of permanent well-paying jobs. But what is the probability of such changes, in the context of the Mexican political system as it exists today? Improving the livelihoods of small peasant farmers in most parts of the country would involve a harsh, sustained attack upon local *caciques,* exploitative commercial middlemen, and others at the local and regional level who prey upon the small farmer. But these "exploiters" also serve as key agents of political control and mobilization for the Mexican government; in many areas, they are the "institutional pillars" of the regime. Eliminating them in order to increase peasant incentives for greater production and boost employment would carry major political costs and risks for any Mexican administration.

Finally, if major changes in political and economic structures are essential to a frontal attack on the poverty/unemployment problem, how tolerable would such changes be, from the U.S. point of view? Richard Fagen of Stanford University reports that U.S. government officials and businessmen whom he interviewed in the fall of 1977 regarded precipitous changes in Mexican politics and economics as "unacceptable," although there was no consensus on what could or should be done in case "unacceptable" changes began to take place. He also notes that the more important Mexican oil becomes to the United States, the broader the definition of "unacceptable" will tend to become. Is the U.S. willing to support a truly serious tax reform in Mexico? A basic shake-up of the land tenure system? Withdrawal of subsidies to large-scale agribusiness operations? Financial penalties for businesses that insist on locating investments in Mexico City rather than the hinterlands, where they tend to be more job-creating? Vigorous and uniform enforcement of the official minimum wage? The unleashing of the country's now largely captive labor unions? In short, are U.S. political and business elites willing to support the kinds of changes that might set into motion a process that neither the U.S. nor the Mexican government might be able to control completely and which might weaken or eliminate some basic features of the Mexican development model that have been highly functional to the expansion of U.S. investment and trade with Mexico? These are the kinds of questions that rarely surface in discussions about using U.S. immigration policy as a blunt instrument to compel Mexican elites to come to grips with poverty and unemployment in their country.

Policy Options

What more could be done, within existing political and economic constraints, to increase the labor-absorptive capacity of the Mexican economy? The main policy options for the short run relate to the mix and coverage of rural development programs, including food-processing industry (*agroindustrias*). In the medium to long term, there may be considerable room for expansion of small-scale, labor-intensive, nonagriculturally based consumer goods industries. I shall sketch these options briefly and relate them to current programs and policies being pursued by the Mexican government.

As the Lopez Portillo administration entered its final two-and-a-half years, rural development funds were being channeled through five major, partially overlapping, partially competing programs: PIDER (*Programa de Inversiones para el Desarrollo Rural*), begun in 1973; CUC (*Convenios Únicos de Coordinación*), begun in 1977; COPLA-MAR (*Programa Coordinador para las Zonas Marginadas*), begun in 1977; *Distritos de Temporal,* also initiated in 1977; and SAM (*Sistema Alimentario Mexicano*), announced in March 1980. All these programs share some of the same objectives (increasing the productivity of small farms through irrigation, technology, credit, and other inputs; improving rural infrastructure, especially feeder roads; extending social services, especially schools, health clinics, and potable water systems; generating new temporary and permanent employment; and improving nutrition and income distribution). They also tend to concentrate their investments in many of the same local areas (micro-regions, municipios críticos, etc.) and the same state (especially

Oaxaca, Guerrero, Zacatecas, Durango, Chiapas, and the Yucatán).
There are, however, some important differences in emphasis among
these five rural-sector programs. The PIDER program places relatively greater stress on permanent employment creation, mainly
through small-scale irrigation works, than the others. COPLAMAR,
which will spend over $3 billion during the 1980–82 period, is a "basic
needs" development program stressing social infrastructure (clinics,
feeder roads, potable water), food distribution, and assistance in com-
mercializing agricultural products. It has no "production" component.
The CUC system is a federal to state and local government revenue
sharing program which finances mainly rural road and school construction. The *Distritos de Temporal* program, based in the Ministry
of Agriculture and Water Resources, is aimed at boosting the productivity of small farms in areas of rainfall-dependent agriculture
through agricultural extension, research, and credit services, as well
as some infrastructure investments, a soil and water conservation program, and reforestation projects. SAM, which is supposed to encom-
pass several if not all of the aforementioned rural development
programs, seeks nothing less than the total rejuvenation of the small-
scale, subsistence sector of Mexican agriculture, with a view toward
increasing the production of basic food grains (corn, beans, rice,
wheat, soya, sorghum) by the small farmers in this sector. The overriding goal of SAM is to achieve national self-sufficiency in production
of these basic crops and reduce Mexico's dependence on imported
food. (In 1980 Mexico found it necessary to import from the United
States some 11 million metric tons of foodstuffs, worth over $2 billion.)
The main policy instruments to be employed are more generous
official crop support prices for corn and beans (to be raised by 50
percent); liberalized credit (with interest rates for corn and bean
cultivation to be reduced from 14 to 3 percent); more ample crop
insurance; low-cost seeds, fertilizers, and insecticides; and steps to
bring new lands under cultivation. New jobs are to be generated by
these measures to stimulate agricultural production, particularly in
areas of rainfall-dependent agriculture, and by public and private
investments in food-processing industries. The program also seeks to
improve the nutritional level of 35 million Mexicans living in impoverished rural communities and urban squatter settlements.

Critics of "social infrastructure" programs like COPLAMAR, CUC,
and, to a lesser extent, the *Distritos de Temporal* program argue that

such investments do not leave enough of a residue of permanent employment and that the numerous temporary jobs (mostly in construction) that they do create often serve only to make peasants more dependent on wage-labor, cash income. They thus become more prone to migrate, in search of cash income-earning opportunities. Shifting the mix of public investment toward tube-well irrigation projects, agroindustries, and nonagriculturally-based rural industries would increase the rate of permanent employment creation in the countryside. In addition to its undesirable "side effects," temporary employment has very weak multiplier effects in terms of permanent job creation. According to one estimate, it takes ten man-years of temporary work (e.g., in construction of federally-funded road-building projects) to create one new permanent rural job.

There is, however, considerable skepticism about the capacity of agroindustries to provide permanent employment for more than a small minority of the rural population. Proponents of the SAM system claim that, in addition to those workers directly employed, each job created in the food-processing industry will generate five to six jobs in agricultural production. Critics contend that this employment impact is greatly exaggerated. And while there have been some highly successful small-scale textile and garment factories observed in Mexican rural communities, the outlook for other types of nonagriculturally-based rural industries remains problematic. Most of the rural industries established under the PIDER program and the now-defunct FONAFE (*Fondo Nacional de Fomento Ejidal*) program seem to have failed, and the large private sector firms have little interest in this type of development. Thus the prospects for nonagricultural rural employment creation are not encouraging.

The establishment and heavy funding of programs like SAM and the *Distritos de Temporal* have shifted government investment in agriculture from an overwhelming emphasis on irrigated areas (75 percent or more of all federal investment in agriculture prior to 1972) toward stimulation of production in areas of rain-fed agriculture. While this new emphasis on rain-fed agriculture will certainly help to achieve the government's objective of national self-sufficiency in basic food grains, the investments in this sector are not expected to generate much new permanent employment. The latter goal might be served better by a public investment strategy emphasizing small-scale irrigation projects.

Within the urban-industrial sector of the economy, greater labor absorptiveness could be achieved by promoting small-scale, labor-intensive, intermediate technology firms producing consumer goods for export, rather than more capital-intensive import-substituting industries and producer goods industry (manufacturing heavy machinery, etc.). But any Taiwan–South Korean-style industrialization strategy emphasizing labor-intensive consumer goods intended primarily for export would depend for its success upon much wider access to the U.S. consumer market. In a period when U.S. protectionist barriers are likely to remain high for most of the consumer goods which Mexico could export, such as shoes and textiles, this export-oriented strategy of job creation seems unrealistic.

There are other, nonsectorial policies that could be pursued to increase the labor-intensity of Mexican development. These include fiscal incentives to employers (subsidies or tax credits for new workers hired; reduced payroll taxes), higher tariffs on imports of capital goods, and greater fiscal incentives to promote decentralization of private investments away from the Mexico City, Guadalajara, and Monterrey metropolitan areas and the northern border corridor toward smaller urban centers in the interior and coastal areas. While some of these measures have already been partially implemented, there is still much room for improvement.

It must be recognized, however, that no matter how many new jobs are created in Mexico during the next twenty years, the huge real-wage differential between Mexico and the U.S. and other factors will continue to drive workers across the border. While interview data suggest that the wage differential would not have to be wiped out—only narrowed—in order to induce some potential migrants to remain in their home communities, others would still migrate because of other kinds of advantages afforded by employment in the U.S. (greater steadiness of income, fewer educational requirements for low-skill occupations than in Mexican cities, and so forth). The importance of these "other factors" in decisions to migrate is highlighted by the finding of most field studies completed to date that only a small proportion (3 to 6 percent) of Mexican migrants to the U.S. had been openly unemployed in their home community just before they went to the U.S. for the first (or most recent) time. While much larger proportions of U.S.-bound migrants had been underemployed, or lacked remunerated employment (e.g., eldest sons helping their fathers on the family farm plot), it is evident that even for many of them, wage differentials, job status differences, and other factors operating in both the sending communities and receiving areas in the U.S. would have caused them to migrate, regardless of local (home community) employment opportunities. In short, solving Mexico's *employment* problem is not the same as solving its *emigration* problem. Reducing unemployment and underemployment will not result in a commensurate decrease in migration to the United States. There is no "one-to-one" relationship.

Conclusion

There is much to be faulted in the development policies pursued by Mexican elites during the last four decades, particularly in the agricultural sector. A variety of public policies that encouraged and subsidized the substitution of capital for labor has engendered a genuine crisis of unemployment and underemployment, which is destined to get worse before it starts to diminish.

Mexico continues to pursue a development strategy that is basically capital-intensive, in which higher priority is attached to building up the oil/petrochemical industry and other heavy industry (steel, cement, fertilizers, heavy machinery) than to promoting small-scale manufacturing industry to produce basic consumer goods. There is, however, more sensitivity to the employment implications of public investments today than there was a decade ago, or even three years ago. With each passing year of the Lopez Portillo administration, there has been slightly more emphasis (at least in government planning) on job creation and a "basic needs" approach to development. For example, the Global Development Plan announced in early 1980 sets more ambitious targets for employment than the National Industrial Development Plan for 1979 to 1990 announced in February 1979. The plan for a "National Food System" (SAM), which was prepared by the President's personal staff of advisors and announced on March 18, 1980, is significantly more poverty/employment/basic needs–oriented than the 1980 agricultural plan drawn up by the Ministry of Agriculture and Water Resources, which continued the government's longstanding emphasis on support for the large-scale, commercial, agriculture sector. Within the industrial sector, government planning now places greater stress on integrating capital-intensive industries with a chain of other, more labor-intensive industries. The highly capital-intensive petrochemical industry, for example, will be linked to the more labor-intensive synthetic fiber, textile, and garment industries.

All this suggests that the internal debate over labor-intensity versus capital-intensity in the government's strategy for investing oil revenues is an on-going debate, that Mexican elites have not lost all touch with social realities in their country, and that there is still genuine interest on the part of at least one segment of the top-level policy-making elite in measures that could significantly increase the labor-intensive capacity of the Mexican economy. It is clear, however, that the regime is not willing to constrain economic growth (especially in the industrial sector) in order to maximize employment creation in the short run. If growth and job creation come into conflict in any given area, the government will opt for maximizing economic growth. There is a clear preference for public investments that will build up the industrial production capacity of the economy and create permanent employment opportunities in that sector of the economy, rather than agriculture, the service sector, or short-term construction projects.

The basic operating premise of Mexican government policy seems to be that the country's employment problems can only be solved in the long run (i.e., in the next generation) and only as a result of urban-industrial development. The overriding goal, in the medium to long run, is to turn today's peasants, and their offspring, into factory operatives with more secure, better-paid employment. In this policy context, the "oil bonanza" must not be squandered on temporary make-work projects, income transfer programs, and other kinds of "welfare schemes" (*subsidios a la miseria*) for the rural and urban poor. Rather, the revenues must be used to build up a much larger base of permanent employment in the urban-industrial sector. Thus, massive, short-term job-creating programs are not in the cards, and *no amount of pressure from the United States will bring them into existence.*

There is, however, a not insignificant degree of movement on the part of the Mexican policy-making elite toward coming to grips with the country's employment problem. Popular rhetoric in the U.S. notwithstanding, Mexican elites—both public and private sector—*do* have an objective interest in policies that will reduce unemployment and underemployment, raise the incomes and living standards of the poor, and diminish emigration to the United States. Even if Mexican elites have no particular interest in stopping the *U.S.–bound* flow of migrants, investments and policies that tend to reduce rural out-migration *generally* will also have the effect of reducing pressures for migration to the United States. The source areas for both internal (rural-to-urban) and U.S.–bound migration are largely overlapping. The region which contributes most to migration to the U.S. also generates more than one-fourth of all internal migrants within Mexico.

The importance of these areas as breeding grounds for migrants to Mexico's largest cities (as well as to the U.S.) has not been lost upon Mexican policy makers. Mexican elites are increasingly alarmed about the uncontrolled growth of Mexico City (population in 1980, about 14 million), owing to continued in-migration from the hinterlands as well as natural population increase among the urban-born. Droughts and other natural disasters continue to drive new waves of migrants out of the countryside into Mexico City and a handful of smaller metropolitan areas. Air pollution, traffic congestion (an estimated 15 million man-hours are lost daily in Mexico City traffic jams), water shortages, and other problems are reaching crisis proportions in these principal cities. There is a very direct, immediate, and increasingly recognized Mexican elite interest in increasing the labor-absorptive capacity of those rural areas and small cities that generate at least 80 percent of Mexico's migrants to the United States.

There is also rising concern among the Mexican political elite that the oil boom will worsen the country's distribution of personal income, which is already one of the most unequal in the world. The expectations and frustrations of the Mexican poor will inevitably rise as the process of income concentration intensifies and high rates of inflation continue to erode their real incomes. As a Mexican official recently told a U.S. reporter, "We've had oil long enough for people to realize that it is doing them no good. Expectations are beginning to appear for which we must find an answer." Mexican policy makers are not suicidal; they can be expected to channel a significant and growing proportion of the revenues from oil and gas exports into the kinds of projects and programs that have the greatest potential impact on poverty and unemployment, if only because to do otherwise would set the stage for political destabilization.

This reallocation of public resources will be incremental, not abrupt. The Mexican government is not likely to abandon its basic developmental strategy of "growth first, permanent (mainly industrial) jobs later." Even in the rural sector, programs like SAM are basically a governmental response to Mexico's crisis of agricultural production

—its inability to feed itself, without massive, costly foreign food imports—rather than a frontal assault on rural poverty and unemployment problems. SAM and its collateral programs may fail to generate much new employment in the "benefited" areas. The billions of pesos being pumped into such programs may only end up further enriching the private agribusiness entrepreneurs, agricultural input suppliers, commercial middlemen, and local *caciques* who have always benefited disproportionately from public investments in the rural sector. But programs like SAM are based on an accurate diagnosis of the nation's agrarian problems and, if fully implemented, would have the effect of increasing the economic viability and labor retention capacity of small-scale agriculture in Mexico.

But the time dimension is critical. It is unrealistic to think that the effects of four decades of official neglect of rain-fed agriculture and small-scale commerce and industry can be swept away overnight. The groups and individuals who have profited handsomely from public policies and institutional arrangements that have strengthened the hand of large-scale producers over that of small producers will not simply go away. They will continue to demand their subsidies, and silencing them will be politically costly, if not prohibitive.

For most groups in the United States, however, solving Mexico's employment, poverty, and income distribution problems in the next generation does not constitute an acceptable Mexican response to what is widely *perceived* to be a highly detrimental migration phenomenon. However erroneous the perception, from the standpoint of U.S. interests, it nevertheless fuels resentment toward Mexico and creates a broad popular constituency for punitive responses by the U.S. government. The man and woman in the street, as well as their elected representatives, now see oil-rich Mexico as a wealthy country that can and should produce a short-term (not just long-term) solution to the migration problem with its own resources. In their view, the U.S. should stop subsidizing capital-intensive development in Mexico and end our "foreign aid" (i.e., employment opportunities in the U.S. for Mexican workers) to that country. The complexities and obstacles to producing a short-term "solution" to this (allegedly) "made-in-Mexico" problem are simply ignored in the U.S. debate concerning immigration from Mexico.

The response of U.S. policy makers to the domestic political imperative to "do something" about the flow of Mexican migrants is increasingly likely to take the form of pressure on Mexico to shift more rapidly to a less capital-intensive strategy of development: to attach higher priority to direct, immediate job creation, even at the expense of higher rates of growth in industrial production and infrastructure.

This places U.S. policy makers on a direct collision course with their Mexican counterparts. The capital-intensity of Mexico's oil investment strategy will therefore be a constant source of tension in U.S.–Mexican relations during the 1980s and beyond. The Mexican government can and should extend and deepen its poverty/employment-oriented development programs. It must be willing to assume the political costs and risks involved in pushing those programs toward full implementation. But no Mexican President could afford, politically, to make radical changes in the country's basic model of development *under overt pressure from the United States*. Given the extreme nationalistic sensitivity that surrounds anything having to do with the Mexican oil industry, dating back to its expropriation from British and U.S. oil companies in 1938, any attempt by the U.S. to bring public pressure to bear on the Mexicans to use their oil export earnings in certain ways will be strongly resisted. Barring the U.S. door to Mexican migrants may thus provide Americans with an outlet for their frustrations, but, as a strategy for effecting changes in Mexico's pattern of development, it is simply naïve and almost certainly counterproductive.

Guido Belsasso *

6

Undocumented Mexican Workers in the U.S.

A Mexican Perspective

Introduction

The purpose of this chapter is to analyze, from a Mexican national perspective, the phenomenon of the migration of Mexican workers to the United States, as well as the policies that both countries have established with respect to the phenomenon throughout the different periods in history.

Migration is not a phenomenon limited to the present, but a universal human activity. In an attempt to transform nature and put it to his own use, man has had to migrate for climatic, geographic, political, economic, or social reasons. Thus, the migratory phenomenon

---

* Translated by Catherine Steele Castro and Sharon Washtien Franco.

GUIDO BELSASSO *is director general of the National Institute of Labor Studies of the Ministry of Labor and Social Welfare in Mexico. He has had a distinguished career as a consultant, lecturer, and professor of psychiatry. Dr. Belsasso has been president of the Mexican Society of Neurology, secretary general and treasurer of the Inter-American Council of Psychiatric Associations, and founder and director general of the Mexican Center for Studies on Drug Abuse. In addition to being on the editorial boards of several medical journals, he is founder and editor of the* Journal of the National Institute of Neurology. *Dr. Belsasso authored* The Psychiatric Care of the Underprivileged *and has contributed chapters to other volumes both in Mexico and abroad.*

assumes diverse dimensions and explanations throughout history. In the case of undocumented workers in the United States, its analysis acquires particular relevance, for far from being an isolated phenomenon, it involves a series of political, economic, and social relations between both countries.

The commitment between the United States and Mexico should concentrate on the correct analysis of the problem in order to define possible policies favorable to resolving it.

With the realization that the problem was multidimensional and that throughout history it had been approached in different ways, a historical analysis of the different explanations, approaches, and policies put forward by both Mexico and the United States was considered necessary. In the analysis of the historical antecedents, the bilateral policies of both countries in the last decade especially stand out. The Mexican approach tends toward an evaluation of specific bilateral problems and their impact on relations between Mexico and the United States in general.

The second section of this document mentions and analyzes some of the partial studies carried out in connection with the magnitude of the migratory problem in the United States. In order to advance these studies, the Mexican government, through the Ministry of Labor and Social Welfare and its National Center for Labor Information and Statistics (CENIET), has, since 1977, evaluated, quantitatively and qualitatively, the flow of migratory workers. This evaluation is based on a National Survey of Migration to the Northern Border and the United States (ENEFNEU).

In the third part of this study I shall bring out considerations within a historical framework, taking into account the importance of the migratory flow and the policies which have been established in that respect.

Finally I shall present the overall conclusions of the document. Such conclusions should help toward an understanding of the migratory phenomenon within the development plan which Mexico wishes to establish, and also to define a correct organization of resources by sector in accordance with the great national objectives which seek, fundamentally, to provide a life of dignity for all Mexican people, on both an individual and a social plane.

In order to understand and place the immigration phenomenon within the context of Mexican-American bilateral relations (this problem being considered in the United States as a political one since the matter is resolved through Congress and the Executive Branch), it is important to take into account some historical antecedents relating to the phenomenon, as well as to draw attention to some aspects of American policy regarding documented and undocumented immigration, and Mexico's position with regard to this policy.

North American Policy Throughout History

The first official statistics on the number of immigrants admitted into the United States date back to 1819. The United States Immigration and Naturalization Service has provided information on the characteristics and patterns regarding sex, age, and occupational antecedents, as well as on migratory sources since 1819. However, for the objectives of this study it is sufficient to say that the large-scale migratory movement from Mexico began at the start of the century and increased, on the one hand, because of the demand for manual labor caused by the departure of American troops abroad during the First World War, and on the other hand, because of the exodus of large numbers of Mexicans who left their country during the revolutionary upheaval which overwhelmed Mexico after the overthrow of the Porfirio Diaz regime.

During the period 1921 to 1940, 67.4 percent of a total of 4.6 million immigrants came from Germany, the United Kingdom, Canada, and Mexico. In the early thirties the Depression caused a decline in immigration. However, during that period the increased immigration of Mexicans began to be considered as a "social problem," and consequently social studies were initiated and projects were financed by the authorities to define the problem. The first permanent law relating to United States migratory quotas was then implemented.

Between 1941 and 1960 immigration continued to decrease, and as a result of postwar legislation the majority of immigrants was composed of "war brides." Mexico, together with Canada and the West Indies, provided 30.4 percent of the total number of immigrants.

In the period 1961 to 1975, the quota system applying to national origin was abolished, and this resulted in a significant increase in the rate of immigration in comparison to previous years, Asian immigration predominating.

In general terms it is worthwhile mentioning the transnational aspects of the migratory phenomenon; the flow of work force from one country to another occurs within specific structural frameworks: property, capital, technology, and culture, among others. Thus, in Europe during the 19th century and at the turn of the 20th century, the effects of the Industrial Revolution spread, causing manpower to leave Europe; this was largely absorbed by the Americas, particularly the United States, a vast country beginning to undergo a process of accelerated development. The prospect of more remunerative work in the agricultural and mine expansion programs, road construction, and railroad maintenance generated a movement which continued to grow until the period of the Depression in the thirties. The new arrivals, deprived of access to higher occupational levels, filled low-level jobs formerly occupied by the local work force.

These then are the principal historical characteristics of legal or documented immigration to the United States since the second decade of the 19th century.

With regard to the evolution of the United States immigration policy, it is interesting to note that the first federal legislation on naturalization was promulgated in 1790, and eight years later Congress approved a series of laws on immigrants and sedition which tended to create antimigratory feeling, especially in the Northwest. However, immigration continued in the period 1830 to 1880, and the migratory flow from Great Britain, Germany, Ireland, and the Scandinavian countries increased considerably.

The first federal law which stimulated immigration was introduced by Congress in 1864 as a result of the shortage of manpower caused by the Civil War. In 1875 Congress approved the first legislation restricting the admission of immigrants to the United States, and in 1882, because of the increase in Chinese immigration, Congress introduced the first Chinese Exclusion Law, which was not repealed until the time of the Second World War. In the same year, 1882, the first general immigration statute was applied; its purpose was to restrict the entry of persons who might prove to be a public burden.

The first law designed to put an end to the practice of importing cheap labor from abroad was promulgated in 1885. Special investigation boards, the requiring of passenger statements to be drawn up upon arrival in the country, and the proliferation of immigration laws have their origin in an 1893 statute. In that year a resolution authorizing the investigation of illegal immigrants who had come to the United States in order to work was sanctioned; four years later a law requiring educational tests for immigrants was approved. In 1903 a new general immigration law, whose purpose was to codify existing laws, was approved, and the categories of undesirable immigrants were increased.

As a result of the increase in Japanese immigration at the beginning of the century, President Roosevelt signed an agreement with Japan which limited the number of workers entitled to enter the United States, and a commission was authorized to study immigration. This commission published the Dillingham report which provided the source for the 1917 law which codified all the statutes referring to the exclusion of immigrants, and laid down new restrictions which declared inadmissible persons from certain areas of China, India, Persia, Burma, Sweden, the Malayan States, part of Russia, Arabia, Afghanistan, and the greater part of the Polynesian Islands and the East Indian Islands. It also required a literacy test which, because of pressure from the agricultural employers, did not apply to Mexicans. In 1920 another law was passed which provided the basis for the deportation of "enemy immigrants" and "immigrants convicted for the violation of war laws."

The first law to limit immigration quantitatively was passed in 1921. This "quota law" limited the number of immigrants—whatever their nationality—to 3 percent of the total persons of that nationality born abroad. It remained in force until 1924 when it was replaced by a second "quota law" which actually contravened the 14th Amendment of the United States Constitution which prohibited discrimination based on race or national origin. This law incorporated the principle of national origin, and thus the Japanese were excluded, as well as other Oriental races which had previously been eliminated. An exception was made which admitted certain foreigners "not subject to quotas," and which was designed to attract Mexican immigrants. In 1924 the Border Immigration Patrol was created.

Between 1932 and 1935, as a consequence of the Depression, the number of people who emigrated from the United States was greater than the number of immigrants entering the country. This situation changed during the forties with the recuperation of the country's economy and the outbreak of fascism and nazism which resulted in a new wave of emigration to the United States.

The 1917 law was amended in 1940; it stipulated that immigrants' fingerprints be recorded and filed, and envisaged clauses concerning the deportation of immigrants convicted of smuggling or of collaborating in the illegal entry of other immigrants. Then the Second World War broke out and immigration decreased, only to increase again after the war. Racial obstacles to immigration and naturalization were suppressed.

1952 was a significant year, for the Immigration and Nationalization Law, still in force today, was enacted. This law revised and codified all the then existing laws on immigration and nationalization. From that time on, the most important legislation on the subject was issued on October 3, 1965; it abolished the quota system based on national origin which had been in force since 1924.

With respect to undocumented immigrants, the United States government has tried, since 1951, to make it a standard offense to employ such persons and has also proposed various bills. Because of the importance for Mexico of the opinions held by different American groups on the migratory issue—such opinions being reflected by their impact on legislative work—I shall refer briefly to the bills presented to Congress in the last decade.

In the 92nd Congress, a subcommittee carried out a congressional investigation which included members of Congress, public officials, union representatives, employers' associations, religious and civil groups, ethnic and minority groups, social service agencies, and documented and undocumented immigrants. It was concluded that undocumented immigrants had an undeniable negative effect on the economy, and a law proposed to protect American workers was approved by the House of Representatives on September 12, 1972. In the 93rd Congress it was proposed once again, and approved with an amendment on May 3, 1973.

In the 94th Congress further amendments were incorporated whose objectives were to strengthen the project against arguments of labor discrimination and to favor the regularization of the migratory status of those undocumented immigrants who had developed substantial interests during their residence in the United States. In the same Congress, Representative Peter Rodino of New Jersey presented a bill for the third time, although it was not approved by the Senate. It proposed, as did other bills concerned with Mexican immigration to the United States, the application of sanctions to those employers who knowingly hired undocumented migratory workers, and also the possibility of regularizing the migratory status of undocumented workers who had lived in the United States for the period of five years, and who had not been a public burden.

Democrat and Republican representatives in favor of the Rodino bill have maintained the opinion that the hiring of undocumented immigrants by employers with knowledge before the fact should be regarded as an illegal activity; this bill refers to those whose migratory status prohibits them from accepting employment. Supporters of the bill base their argument on the unjust competition that American workers have to contend with, and the grave consequences for the United States economy in general, since the problem is not limited to agriculture but has extended to industry and commerce; neither is it limited to the southern border, but has extended to the principal metropolitan areas.

The arguments put forward against this bill, again by representatives of both parties, maintain that the bill is highly discriminatory, for it places difficult responsibilities on the employers who have to decide as to the citizenship or migratory status of the persons. Furthermore it denies the possibility of a cheap manual labor market and encourages the violation of the basic rights and the human dignity of both immigrants and citizens, as well as the cruel and unnecessary separation of families.

The Mexican-American groups consider that this type of legislation would act as an incentive for racist employers to deny "Chicanos" job opportunities.

In various states of the country, laws similar to the one proposed by Rodino have been approved, but constitutional experts predict that, as long as the federal government reserves the right to legislate on immigration, there will be conflicts in their application.

In the 95th Congress, among the outstanding bills is one which contains, along with other postulations, the laying down of proceedings which would enable the Social Security Administration, in association with the Attorney General, to prevent undocumented workers from receiving social security cards; a bill which stipulates as a condition for obtaining official approval from each state governor for the employment of temporary foreign workers, the employment of citizens on a priority basis in agricultural work; a bill which eliminates the condition of five-years residence in the country in order to benefit from the state medical program; and other bills of even greater importance relating to the refugee program.

Other bills before the House of Representatives propose: the sanctioning of employers; the establishment of a Select Commission on Immigration and Refugee Policy and a Presidential Commission on Immigrant Policy between Mexico and the United States; amnesty by documentation which would extend a change of status to those who have entered the United States on or before January 1, 1977; the collection of salaries owed by employers of undocumented workers. Mention should also be made of the bill which classifies as an offense, punishable by deportation, the obtaining by immigrants of unemployment compensation, public aid, and other federal benefits; the bill stipulating the registration of the granting of permanent resident status to those who entered the country before July 4, 1976, excluding those guilty of criminal offenses or subversive behavior or those whose financial position is unstable; the bill which proposes stronger sanctions for illegal entry, and additional border control.

Finally there is the bill which stipulates that any immigrant who has been detained for subsequent investigation or who has been temporarily expelled from the United States has the right to be legally represented, and the bill which states that any immigrant who becomes a public burden within twenty-four months of his arrival in the country will be subject to deportation.

With reference to the bills presented in the 96th Congress, an analysis of the propositions reveals two positions—a hard line and a moderate one. Charles B. Keely in his study "Immigrants in the United States: A Political Analysis," observes that three perspectives stand out in the debate in the 96th Congress.

1. *Modifying American migratory policy to adjust the migratory flow according to work force requirements.* Supporters of this position say that the workers, whether documented or not, displace American workers and so exacerbate the unemployment phenomenon, besides being a public burden which harms the national economy. They suggest reinforcing the border patrol; establishing more rigid requisites for the granting of labor, social security, and public assistance credentials, and the sanctioning of both employers who hire "undocumented workers," and workers who provide false information. The AFL-CIO is the principal group supporting this trend. However, they do not

have the complete support of the American labor groups who, while they do not favor the expansion of programs which permit entry to foreign workers, do prefer legal preventive measures to repressive ones. Such is the case with the Chicano labor groups.

2. *Establishing a migratory policy with adequate restrictions on immigration in order to control the population growth in the United States.* The reasoning behind this position is based on the fallacy that the immigration flow is a major factor in the population growth in the United States, and that this will jeopardize the health of the environment in the future. Supporters of this position favor preventing immigration by strengthening the border patrol and the labor laws, sanctioning employers, and channeling necessary aid to the exterior in order to control the birth rate and to create employment which would retain possible future immigrants in their own country. The principal promoters are Zero Population Growth and the Environmental Fund.

3. *Drawing up labor policies on immigration which favor the reuniting of families and the admission of refugees.* The groups which support this alternative reject the notion that immigration has a negative effect on the United States, and consider that a limited and selective policy is unacceptable. They support the implementation of a liberal policy with regard to migratory questions which, while permitting the unification of the family nucleus, would maintain the humanitarian tradition of this country with regard to the admission of refugees. Various refugee and immigrant aid groups, ethnic organizations, and religious groups support this position.

Besides the positions indicated by Keely, a fourth one may be added whose purpose is to strengthen the programs concerned with the temporary hiring of foreign workers, and which is based on the realistic needs of innumerable American farms.

When a country is undergoing a period of electoral excitement, the confrontation of attitudes assumed by different groups is necessarily reflected in the bills which congressional members attempt to have approved, and such was the case with regard to the migration issue during the 96th American Congress. There were several bills whose principal objectives reflect the hard line position. These objectives are:

—Make illegal the deliberate employment of undocumented foreigners.

—Grant social security cards in order to identify foreigners unable to obtain employment.

—Deport foreigners who, through mental or physical disabilities, have become a public burden.

—Exact greater requisites for the hiring of temporary foreign workers.

—Deport foreigners who participate in violent or illegal action related to political matters.

—Coordinate the Immigration and Naturalization Service and the Department of Health to facilitate the deportation of any foreigner who receives aid for more than six months.

—Refuse admission to immigrants who do not make a previous declaration of financial support for the period of five years.

—Approve the "Control of Foreigners Law" which proposes strengthening the border patrol and new methods for detecting the entry of undocumented immigrants; facilitate the admission of temporary workers whenever all internal legal means have been exhausted; limit the authorization of social security cards; prevent the authorization of any financial aid to associations which provide work opportunities, training, and education to "illegal" foreigners.

The bills which support the "moderate" position propose the following:

—Guarantee that detained migrants be represented by lawyers.

—Establish programs permitting the entry of Mexicans to work temporarily.

—Establish programs permitting workers to enter under specific contract.

—Establish visa programs for Mexican workers; temporary permission for a six-month period; determine the number of visas in relation to the number of unfilled jobs; give permanent resident status to those foreigners who have resided in the United States for a long time.

In conclusion it can be stated that the criteria of different members of Congress vary with respect to the migratory problem.

The bills presented demonstrate the persistence of the idea that the foreign workers, especially the undocumented workers, constitute a threat for the American workers. It is maintained that not only do they displace American workers, but also that they have an adverse effect on the salary rate and the work conditions. Foreign workers are then a heavy burden on the American economy in that they exacerbate the unemployment problem and absorb significant social security benefits.

However, it is important to point out that there is a developing trend in opinion which analyzes the problem from a more objective point of view, considering the immigration of workers to be caused not by unemployment in other countries, but rather by the attraction which the supply in the American labor market has for them; in the final count the employers are the ones who benefit from the conditions in which these workers are hired. Charles Keely has this to say: "There will be many actors with conflicting interests and much activity in different forums before substantial changes in American legislation become a reality."

Actions Taken by President Carter's Administration

In his message to Congress on August 4, 1977, President Carter referred to undocumented immigration and proposed a legislative policy on two levels: the first, dealing with "amnesty," defined his concern for the social situation of undocumented workers, and the second, dealing with "restriction," would introduce a control belt along the border to restrict the immigration of undocumented workers.

The first proposal referred to the possibility of extending immigrant resident status to all undocumented workers who had lived continuously in the United States from January 1, 1970, up until the date of the message. The foreigners would apply for this status by producing proof of residence, and if they continued doing this for five years, they could then apply for American citizenship.

Another possibility, related to "amnesty," was the provision for all undocumented workers—excluding those classified as exchange immigrants or visiting students—who had lived in the United States since before January 1, 1977, to choose temporary residential status for the period of five years; however, they would not be permitted to vote, occupy public positions, or bring their families to live with them, and, unlike permanent residents, they would not be entitled to federal social services.

Finally, undocumented workers who had entered the country after January 1, 1977, would not be able to obtain any kind of residential status, and would be subject to the migration laws.

With respect to "restriction," it was proposed that the hiring of undocumented workers be considered illegal, and that employers be sanctioned with fines of $1,000 per worker; methods of control would be strengthened at the border and at other entry points; the governments of those countries which provided the greatest source of undocumented workers would be encouraged to cooperate, and an effort would be made to improve their economies and to exercise more control over immigration traffic rings.

Carter's proposal was rejected and Congress responded by creating the Select Commission for Immigration and Refugee Policy in May 1978. Its primary function was to evaluate the policies, laws, and processes which regulate the admission of immigrants and refugees into the Untied States, and to provide appropriate administrative and legislative recommendations to the President and to Congress. It was also hoped that the conclusions would form a basis for a new policy on the matter.

However, it should be mentioned that before the commission was established, several proposals for the amendment of the Nationality and Immigration Law were presented in different government departments, all of which attempted to provide alternative solutions to the problem of undocumented Mexican migration. It was precisely as a result of these proposals that the trend toward a new *bracero* agreement arose. But an agreement of this nature would be difficult, as the experience of twenty-three years of such agreements had demonstrated; furthermore, the reimplementation of such a policy would remove protection from many immigrants and lead to more repressive measures.

Besides the efforts made by both governments, the H-2 program on the temporary hiring of foreign workers has acquired importance. At the same time it has produced diverse reactions, above all in Spanish-speaking organizations, who argue that this system of hiring is harmful to citizens and residents of Hispanic descent in the United States since the availability of foreigners limits the negotiating power of the labor groups, and generates the existence of a subclass which, because of its status, is limited in the exercising of its rights.

Among the basic concepts and procedures for the employment of foreign temporary workers in the above mentioned H-2 program, there are several which emphasize that the Immigration and Nationality Law has among its objectives the following: that of protecting American workers from the adverse competition which the foreign work force could create, and that of reducing the negative economic effects which could result from a shortage of manpower in unpredictable and rare circumstances.

The different types of "temporary admission" considered in the Immigration Law are: the admission of highly qualified foreigners for a period of less than a year; the admission of workers to occupy jobs for which there are no available nationals, or which no nationals want to occupy; provisional admission of persons employed by transnational companies who are being transferred from one post to a similar one.

Of the opinions on the H-2 program expressed before the Select Commission, those of the employers and labor groups stand out. The former favor the strengthening of the program and the application of "liberal criteria" in its implementation, while the labor groups have strongly rejected the program because of the adverse implications it would have for American workers. These apparently irreconcilable opinions make it difficult for the Mexican government to adopt a position on the H-2 program. However, it can be said that Mexico will continue to maintain its traditional position which defends the human and working rights of Mexican workers, whatever their migratory situation.

The creation of a Select Commission on Immigration and Refugee Policy represents the most significant attempt, at a presidential and congressional level, to examine the United States immigration laws and the policies concerning immigration and admission of refugees into the country.

One of the most important and prominent themes included in the studies carried out by the commission is that which refers to "illegal immigrants." It is affirmed that even taking into account the fact that many people enter the United States illegally under the pressure of different problems, no form of illegality can be excused, and the question is raised as to how far it is possible to improve preventive measures on illegal immigration, taking into account the great difficulty of their implementation.

A research plan has been set up to collect the latest information on the impact of immigrants and refugees on the United States and also to evaluate the nature and magnitude of migratory pressures on the United States foreign policy and to assess the different research studies made on the subject.

The first report takes into account the fact that the recommendations must be made on the basis of essentially fragmentary information. The most important general conclusions resulting from the first months of study are:

—There are probably no more than six million illegal immigrants in the United States, perhaps less in certain periods.
—There are probably no more than three million illegal Mexican migrants in the United States, perhaps less in certain periods.
—Very few complete research studies have been made on the impact of recent migrations and the recent arrival of refugees in the country.
—The population growth rate in the United States is determined to a limited extent by the relative changes in the fertility level, in comparison with the substantial changes caused by immigration.

In their report, the commission presented some points of a general nature which are included below.

—The racism and xenophobia which once characterized the opposition to immigration in the United States have not undergone a significant change in the mass media.
—Although there is sympathy for the refugees, there is also an awareness of their impact.
—Strong support in favor of reuniting families has been shown, but at the same time there is a strong current of opposition in favor of certification of temporary work.
—Strong popular opinion considers that illegal immigrants have a negative effect on the economy, although many experts do not share this idea.
—Some people believe that legalization of the immigrant situation would be the correct solution to the problems mentioned above.
—There is growing support in favor of creating a card system which would authorize foreigners to work in the United States, and thus discourage illegal migration.
—The efficiency of the Immigration and Naturalization Service has been widely criticized, and the imposing of sanctions on persons who smuggle workers into the country has been favored.

Mexican Policy

During General Porfirio Diaz's government, emigration was considered to have a positive value; at that time people talked of the advantages the return of the workers to Mexico provided, for they brought with them new skills and better techniques. Later, at the close of the twenties, with the return of the anthropologist Manuel Gamio, who had made some magnificent studies on the subject, people in Mexico began to become more aware of the issue, but the exodus of workers continued to be regarded as an "escape valve," a solution rather than a problem.

In the period between 1934 and 1940, during President Lázaro Cárdenas's term of office, this view changed and the issue became a dominant one. The people's sense of awareness, slight in previous years, became more acute; and the deportation of large contingents of workers, along with the abuses, maltreatment, and violence they suffered, attracted attention and united public opinion, which demanded that the Mexican government protest to the United States government.

Meanwhile, President Lázaro Cárdenas initiated a repatriation program designed to place the deportees in agricultural and cattle raising communal centers. At the same time, the expropriation of the oil, which stimulated the process of industrialization in the country, helped to alleviate the problem.

Later, during Manuel Avila Camacho's administration (1940–1946), at the outbreak of the Second World War—in which both countries were involved—the United States Defense Department requested Mexican workers to fill the vacancies in agriculture, industry, and the public services. The ensuing mobilization of large contingents of workers gave rise to the *bracero* programs in 1942, which terminated twenty-two years later.

The first of these programs, initiated on August 4, 1942, authorized the employment of Mexicans in railroad maintenance. In 1943, 1948, and 1949, agreements were signed authorizing the employment of agricultural workers. Moreover, in 1948, the governments of Mexico and the United States agreed to prohibit the entry of "wetbacks" into the United States, and in 1951, a final agreement of a general nature was signed which was to regulate the situation of Mexican workers until 1964.

From this date onward, the issue of migratory workers was not debated, nor did it occur in any bilateral discussions. However, despite the decrease in legal emigration, the number of persons subject to deportation increased so that from 1961 to 1970 the number of deportees reached 756,000, rose to 934,000 in the period 1972–1973, and rose to 921,000 in 1977.

If the establishment of these *bracero* programs provided a partial solution to the situation, it also generated problems, particularly with regard to illegal immigration, since many Mexicans, hoping to be employed, entered the neighboring country without the required documents. The Mexican government was faced with the necessity of creating a department to deal with selection, hiring, transport, costly board and lodging, and more effective methods of controlling the workers who did not travel in accordance with the fixed "quotas."

The *bracero* program was terminated in 1964 under President Kennedy's administration. It was argued that it had affected the salaries, work conditions, and job opportunities of American citizens. But at the same time, an effort was made to find bilateral formulas and policies of a less aggressive nature than those which had been in existence up to that date. Of course, in that period, the presence of undocumented immigrants in the United States was beginning to be treated as a political question, while in Mexico it was practically ignored.

During Luís Echeverría's administration (1970–1976), the question began to acquire relevance. During their meeting with American authorities in Washington on June 15 and 16, 1972, Echeverría and his secretary of foreign affairs presented in frank terms the problem of the undocumented immigrants, and it was decided to compile information with regard to the question.

The communiqué signed by the leaders of both countries and issued on the same date states among other things:

> . . . with regard to the problems of Mexican migratory workers, the two Presidents analyzed the economic, social, and political factors in the two countries which cause the phenomenon, and agreed on the immediate necessity for each government to study the question with a view to finding a mutually satisfying solution. . . .

In order to attend to this point of the communiqué and at the proposal of Secretary of Foreign Affairs Emilio O. Rabasa, Echeverría ordered the creation of an intersecretarial commission, set up by Rabasa himself, on July 31, 1972. It was called the Intersecretarial Commission for the Study of Clandestine Emigration of Mexican Workers to the United States, and it was composed of representatives from the Ministry of the Interior (Gobernación), the Ministry of Foreign Affairs, the Ministry of Labor and Social Welfare, the Ministry of Education, and the Department of Agrarian Affairs and Colonialization of the Land. At a later date advisers from the Treasury and the Attorney General's office were incorporated.

This commission was to be responsible for the study, evaluation, and analysis of the problems relating to the emigration of Mexican workers to the United States, for the drawing up of a report, and for the proposal of practical and feasible measures to be applied toward solving these problems or, at least, toward improving the situation.

In November of that year, at the request of the United States, informal talks between officials of both countries were held in the Mexican Department of Foreign Affairs, for the purpose of exchanging information and analyzing the problems. At that time each government presented the studies that it had completed with an eye toward resolving the problem.

The assistant attorney general of the United States, Roger Cramton, declared that his country had proposed three objectives:

—To continue and improve good relations with the Mexican government.
—To reduce the number of undocumented workers and to have regard for the consequences suffered by Americans of Mexican descent, as well as the maltreatment and the exploitation of immigrants.
—To improve the treatment of all those inside the United States, including those who enter "illegally."

Cramton pointed out that in order to achieve these objectives, the American government had taken certain measures, for example, legislative amendments, the concession of "voluntary exit" to detained workers, facilities to legalize the situation of those workers who had lived a certain time in the country, and others.

For their part, the members of the commission expressed the Mexican government's concern about the problems resulting from emigration and stressed the words of President Echeverría in his report of September 1, 1972:

The national conscience is disturbed by the emigration of Mexican workers to the United States. Above all we are worried by the unjust and at times inhuman treatment to which they are subjected. . . . We are convinced that the basic solution is to be found within our own borders. . . . We wish to export products and not social problems. . . .

Despite the discrepancies between the positions of the two governments, the conversations proved to be fruitful and points of agreement were reached, among which were to attempt to reduce the number of undocumented workers and to recognize the suitability and necessity of continuing the studies.

Later, prior to the meeting of Presidents Ford and Echeverría in Arizona in October 1975, the Mexican President studied in detail the history of the *bracero* agreements. On the day of the meeting, President Echeverría informed the American President that the Mexican government had no wish to renew such agreements. The new thesis—strengthened by the Mexican public's reaction to the "Hanigan Case" —emphasized the protection of the human and labor rights of the undocumented workers.

> Although in the past our government has tried to solve the problem by means of agreements, this is no longer possible. It must be taken into account that the conditions of both countries are changing rapidly, that our development has been different and consequently requires an attitude of flexibility; dialogue between the two neighboring nations is indispensable.

Actions Taken by the Lopez Portillo Administration

On his first trip to Washington, in February 1977, Lopez Portillo defined his position as one of defense of the dignity of the Mexican and respect for his rights as a worker. At the same time, he pointed out that a new *bracero* agreement would not resolve the problem, as it would only legitimize a few workers and leave many in worse conditions.

In his annual address to the nation on September 1 of that year, he stated:

> We would hope that Mexicans could realize their maximum personal and social potential in our country. Nevertheless, several thousand Mexican workers in search of other horizons cross our borders without the necessary documentation. In part, this movement is a result of our unemployment. I repeat that they are not delinquents; that the possible violation of migration laws does not sanction the infringement of labor laws, and even less of human rights. Therefore we hope that the response to the workers is not police action but measures based on understanding and courtesy among the affected parties in order to resolve this common problem, which

is rooted in a very old relationship between us which is unfavorable to us. To correct it would remedy many ills. We have tried our best to locate the causes and moderate the effects of the problem. We state once more that we want to export not labor but products. Our being able to do so depends on how well we understand the problem and how balanced a solution we can find.

In his address of September 1, 1978, Lopez Portillo stated:

The situation of Mexican laborers who work outside of the country without the required migratory documentation is reason for national concern. Mexican policy on this matter is clear: we will continue to assert that the laborers are men in search of employment, not delinquents, and that completely apart from their migratory situation, their human rights and their labor rights should be recognized and respected.

On September 1, 1979, he made the following statement:

From a multilateral point of view, we maintained active participation in the international bodies to which Mexico belongs. Various proposals were presented, among the most notable that of preparing in the United Nations a code of conduct on the rights of migratory workers.

In the joint communiqué issued by the two Presidents after their meeting of February 14–16, 1979, they stated their commitment to close bilateral cooperation which would make possible an overall realistic solution that respected human dignity and rights. In addition, they agreed to consult one another and meet to share research and studies.

Dimensions of the Problem

In the last ten years there have been several studies of the volume, of workers that cross daily into the United States from Mexico's northern border. Because of the methods used, most of these studies produce fragmentary results. Since 1977, the Mexican government, working through the National Center of Labor Information and Statistics (CENIET) of the Ministry of Labor and Social Welfare, has been developing a program which has as one of its principal objectives the qualitative and quantitative determination of this migratory flow. Below, I will briefly analyze some of the studies conducted in the last decade in the United States and compare the figures provided by these studies with those that have been obtained in Mexico through the National Survey on Emigration to the Northern Border and to the United States (ENEFNEU).

ANALYSIS OF THE STUDIES CARRIED OUT IN THE U.S.

David Heer—The specific objective of David Heer's study was the determination of the total flow of undocumented Mexicans for the period 1970–1975. Working with the population of Mexican origin, Heer used the method of residual calculation, based on several hypotheses:

—The organic growth of the United States population of Mexican descent.
—The social growth as a result of documented immigration.
—The organic growth of the immigrant population.
—The remainder.

Heer presents the possibility of obtaining various estimates which range from 82,000 to 131,000 undocumented workers per year. The estimate considered to be the most reliable is that which is based on the hypothesis that 30 percent of those workers admitted legally return to Mexico and that the Current Population Survey (CPS) underrecords the population of Mexican origin by 10 percent, indicating an annual net flow of 116,000 undocumented workers for 1970–1975.

For lack of information, Heer based his calculation of the birth and death rates of the population of Mexican descent on models, assuming that the CPS records a large part of the undocumented population, and took into account various hypotheses about the volume of the return flow of documented Mexicans. These hypotheses have not been proved. Another limitation of his study is that the CPS population information is limited to habitual residents of the United States. Therefore, it is probable that his figure for the net growth of the undocumented population is overestimated.

Lesko and Associates—In 1976 Lesko and associates undertook a study with the main objective of determining the overall number of undocumented workers. Their estimates were based on indirect methods which made use of two sources of information. For information before 1970, they used a paper by Howard Goldberg on a demographic study. For the 1970s they used as their base the opinions of seven experts of the INS under the following assumptions: that a fixed proportion of those workers who entered the country were apprehended, and that of the successful undocumented Mexicans only 2 percent returned to Mexico of their own choice. The authors indicated that the number of undocumented workers came to a total of between 4.2

million and 11 million, with a probable average of 8.2 million, among which were included 5.2 million Mexicans.

The basic limitation of this study is that the estimates were based on mere speculations, since there were no available empirical data. The results are dependent on the content of the two hypotheses. The calculation of 8.2 million undocumented workers was obtained by averaging the figures indicated by the seven experts in two separate interviews. They represent a subjective appraisal of the size of the undocumented population.

INS—In 1976 the Immigration and Naturalization Service made an exploratory study, the results of which, extrapolated, indicate 500,000 illegal entries into the country at its southern border in 1975. The study's validity is doubtful since it is based on small case studies and the sampling system is unknown. Furthermore, there was no system of control to determine if these entries were of Mexican citizens exclusively.

Joseph A. Reyes and Associates—The central objective was an estimate of the number of undocumented workers residing in the United States, their principal demographic characteristics (sex, age, nationality, and country of origin), and their degree of participation in American public welfare programs and in the labor market.

The technique used was a survey with the following geographical coverage: California, Texas, Michigan, Illinois, Indiana, Ohio, North Carolina, Massachusetts, Pennsylvania, New York, and New Jersey. The original size of the sample was 100,000 homes. Later it was reduced to ten thousand.

The results are unknown; they were never distributed. The only conclusion they reached was that this phenomenon could be measured solely by indirect means.

Clarise Lancaster and Frederick Scheuren—In 1978 another study was conducted to attempt to measure the stock of undocumented workers in the United States. The method used by the authors was the collection and re-collection of data, a method which is used when it is not possible to perform a census. They estimated the population which fell outside of the census, this population having been projected in 1973, and using this method they made an analysis, taking into account the family unit as it was found registered in the Social Security Administration and the Internal Revenue Service. According to the authors, the population calculated in this way was made up of undocumented workers.

The results obtained by this method are the following: the total number of undocumented workers between eighteen and forty-four years of age of all nationalities in April 1973 should be between 2.9 and 5.7 million. Of these, those of the white race, in which Mexicans are included, were estimated to be from 2 to 3.7 million.

J. Gregory Robinson—This author estimated the net undocumented migration using the trend of the mortality rate in ten states of the United States. The difference between the number of deaths suggested by the model and the number of actual deaths provided an estimate of the deaths attributable to the undocumented workers. Later, using the unexpected increase in deaths, Robinson estimated the increase in the size of the stock.

He suggests that the undocumented population between 1960 and 1975 increased from 577,000 to 4,673,000 for white men from twenty to forty-four years of age in the ten states he considered, with an increase from 374,000 to 2,499,000 in the fifteen years after 1960, and an estimated increase from 310,000 to 1,784,000 for 1970–1975.

This study supposes a certain independence among the records which evidently does not exist, a situation which the author tries to compensate for by allowing for a wide margin of error. The estimates were based on assumptions that were unproved and open to criticism. The author himself indicates the speculative character of the study.

MEXICAN STUDIES

In August 1977, Secretary of Labor and Social Welfare Pedro Ojeda Paullada requested and received President Lopez Portillo's consent to carry out a research program that would permit a qualitative and quantitative evaluation of the problem. Thus the Border Studies Program was created, which would provide a data bank of social, economic, and demographic information about the country's northern border zone.

A great deal of the information which has been handled by the U.S. press is mere speculation. A large number of the studies realized in the U.S. are estimates based on the number of arrests made by migration authorities. The figures have been applied with great flexibility, from Lesko's studies, which speak of eight million, to those of Heer, which speak of 82,000 immigrants for 1975.

As stated earlier, the Mexican sources for measuring undocumented migration are the Population Census and the surveys conducted by the CENIET. The CENIET has performed three surveys.

1. The National Survey of Emigration to the Northern Border and to the United States (ENEFNEU).
2. Measurement of the labor flow in the border zone of Baja California.
3. Cost-benefit analysis of the program and its socioeconomic effects on industrial workers and their families.

It is clear that in this chapter interest is basically in the first project; therefore it will be presented in detail.

The objectives of the ENEFNEU are the following:

estimate the migratory flow of Mexican manpower to the United States and its principal characteristics;
estimate the internal migration of the Mexican population and, above all, the migration to the country's northern border and its principal characteristics; and
estimate the volume of the nonmigratory Mexican population and its principal characteristics.

The ENEFNEU is comprised of four stages. The first stage refers to the First Survey of Undocumented Mexican Laborers Repatriated by the United States. Its purpose was to obtain information about the workers' place of residence in Mexico in order to divide the country into regions. The second stage refers to the Second Survey of Undocumented Mexican Laborers Repatriated by the United States, for the purpose of confirming the results of the first survey and verifying the sampling frame and the working hypotheses for the national survey. The third stage is related to the National Migration Survey. The fourth stage refers to a third survey whose objective is to increase the pool of information on undocumented laborers in order to make comparisons with some variables of the National Migration Survey.

The regional breakdown obtained as a result of the first stage was made up of five regions which included all of the states of the Mexican republic. This first survey provided highly interesting data; nevertheless, it is more appropriate to move on to an analysis of the National Migration Survey, conducted from December 1978 to January 1979.

These are preliminary results, and they refer to a population that at that time was working or looking for work in the United States, to be sure; but what is important is that this was the first time that a direct survey, based on a random sample and covering the entire country, was carried out.

The population studied was divided into five groups:

Migrants in the United States.
Migrants who had returned.
Internal border migrants.
Internal nonborder migrants.
Nonmigrant native-born.

The survey made use of a questionnaire applied exclusively to those informants who were working or looking for work in the United States at the time of the interview. The number of laborers was 405,467, a figure which will demonstrate its full meaning when combined with the information about the migrants who had gone to work in the neighboring country and who were in Mexico at the time of the interview. The estimated projections indicate a ceiling of 1.2 million. With these two types of populations it is possible to estimate the number of individuals in the migratory flow.

It is important to take into account the fact that the survey was conducted in the winter, a time when the workers generally return to Mexico, and consequently there are fewer of them in the United States.

The 405,467 workers represent .6 percent of the total population of the country, 1.09 percent of the population of those fifteen years of age or older, and 2.25 percent of the economically active population.

In the first analytical document of the ENEFNEU, the CENIET gives results in three specific areas: profile of the migrants, migratory trends from Mexico to the United States, and internal migration.

PROFILE OF THE MIGRANTS

Of the 405,467 individuals, 346,406 are men (85.4 percent) and 59,061 (14.6 percent) are women, figures that indicate that the migration is eminently masculine, although permanent migration is feminine.

As far as age in concerned, the majority of the migrants are young:

62.4 percent are betwen the ages of fifteen and twenty-nine, and 30.3 percent are between the ages of thirty and forty-nine. The average age is 29.7 years; thus the migrants are considered to be individuals of an age to produce and work and not persons who require education and social and medical assistance.

The educational profile of the migrants is the following: 10.8 percent had not received any instruction; 29.9 percent, from one to three years of elementary education; 44.9 percent, between four and six years; 9.1 percent, from one to three years of secondary education; and only 5.3 percent had completed more than ten years of formal education. The average number of years of education was 4.04 (3.9 for men and 4.7 for women). If this level of education is compared with that of the Mexican population in 1970 (3.1, 3.4, and 2.9, respectively), it can be noted that those who emigrated had a higher educational profile than the national mean.

Although Mexican workers, contrary to what is said in the United States, have a higher level of training than those who remain in the country, their level is lower than that of the Americans, and they are therefore situated in the lower levels of the occupational scale.

The distribution according to marital status revealed that 50.3 percent were unmarried, 47.9 percent married, .7 percent widowed, .4 percent divorced, and .8 percent separated. The high percentage of unmarried individuals implies that at least half of those who emigrate travel without family, and thus suggests that they do not intend to settle in the United States. It could also imply that, lacking economic obligations, they are potential permanent migrants. Nevertheless, the results of the survey with regard to the "economic dependents in Mexico" variable indicate that 57.2 percent of the male migrants support three or more persons, thereby suggesting that the worker emigrates fundamentally in order to obtain higher income and for limited periods of time.

Of the 405,467 persons surveyed, 279,985 (69.1 percent) had sent money to Mexico, especially the unmarried individuals, who sent money in greater proportion than the married ones. This could be due to the fact that it is easier for younger persons to find work, and that unmarried persons may nevertheless have economic dependents. It is necessary to take another factor into account on this point, namely, loans. The data indicate that among those who sent money to Mexico, 49.1 percent had borrowed a certain amount before leaving. Such a situation could be important in the decision of migrants to send money to Mexico, above all to cover debts and the resulting interest.

With respect to the nature of activities carried out before departure for the United States, four categories were considered:

1. Employed persons—worked the month before; had a job but did not work; unpaid family worker.
2. Unemployed persons—did not work but looked for work.
3. Economically inactive persons—pensioners; those dedicated to domestic tasks; students; those incapacitated for work; other activities.
4. Unspecified; unknown.

Seventy-eight percent of the population studied was employed; 3.1 percent unemployed; 15.8 percent economically inactive; and 3.1 percent unspecified. The most important implication of this information is that while the employment situation in Mexico leaves much to be desired, three out of every four migrants had a job before their departure.

Furthermore, knowledge of the type of work they were engaged in is basic for an understanding of the kind of laborers who wish to emigrate. Accordingly, the survey reveals that the primary sector is the main supplier of laborers, since of the 301,582 individuals who worked the month before their departure, 62 percent did so in this sector and 16 percent in the secondary sector. The latter percentage, although not high, deserves attention, since it is comprised of workers with certain skills.

Finally, another factor considered in the profile of the migratory worker is the amount of time that he remains in the neighboring country. The collected data demonstrate that the time of year influences the decision of many individuals not to emigrate. The lowest percentages are of those who, at the time of the interview, had been in the United States from one to twenty-eight days; the highest, among those who had been there from one month to one year. From this information, it can be inferred that the best periods for emigration are the first six months of the year and the summer.

The migrants come fundamentally from seventeen states of the republic, but only those states with the highest percentages will be mentioned (see Table 1). Table 2 shows the migrants' destinations in the U.S.

By means of the ENEFNEU, the CENIET studied one aspect which

TABLE 1.

Guanajuato	17.9 percent
Jalisco	13.9 percent
Chihuahua	12.6 percent
Zacatecas	11.8 percent
Michoacán	8.4 percent
Baja California	5.0 percent
Durango	5.0 percent
San Luis Potosí	4.4 percent

Source: CENIET. National Survey of Emigration to the Northern Border and to the United States, 1978–1979.

TABLE 2.

Destination in the U.S.	Number	Percentage
California	206,522	50.9
Texas	85,953	21.2
Illinois	31,833	7.9
New Mexico	8,190	2.0
Colorado	7,386	1.8
Arizona	6,939	1.7
Oregon	4,897	1.2
Florida	4,336	1.1
Others	16,564	4.1

Source: CENIET. National Survey of Emigration to the Northern Border and to the United States, 1978–1979.

had not been considered before: the migration within the country, which may serve to indicate whether those who emigrated to the neighboring country had previous migratory experience. The data indicate that of the entire population, 13.2 percent were born in a different state from where they were then living; 20.7 percent had had at least one change in place of residence; and 4.9 percent of the labor force which in January 1970 was in Mexico had changed residence within the states of the republic once in nine years. Although the percentages refer to different definitions, they are in agreement on one point: the migrants to the United States had little experience of internal migration.

In conclusion, it is possible to say that the studies carried out in Mexico clearly establish that the basic reasons that migratory workers cross the border are neither unemployment nor lack of education, as has frequently been stated. The educational profile of those who emigrate is higher than the national mean, and 78 percent of those interviewed had jobs when they left for the United States.

Upon analysis, the migratory phenomenon would appear to be the result of a structural situation associated with the growth of the capitalist market system and the evolution of the international economic order. The attraction depends on the difference in salaries in the two countries and some American employers' need for cheap labor.

Conclusion

Throughout this chapter I have considered, within a historical framework, the dimensions of the migratory phenomenon and the associated policies, as analyzed by academic groups as well as official institutions of both countries. The policies and dimensions studied give rise to the following questions:

How can this situation, which has been a problem for the United States for several decades, be resolved?
What measures has each country taken to overcome obstacles and achieve a cooperation based on bilateral interdependence?

In Mexico, the evaluation of the phenomenon is not limited to the concern for the continuous flow of Mexican workers to the United States and the prospect of deportation, nor to exclusive consideration of the protection of their rights independent of their migratory status; Mexico has taken measures to investigate the factors which contribute to the continuation of this migratory movement and also has attempted to find solutions through internal and external policy.

In a spirit of full cooperation, Mexico established a program through the Ministry of Labor and Social Welfare which, in one of its primary stages, made it possible to determine the volume of the migratory flow. This study has destroyed many myths and has scientifically verified that the main reason that workers emigrate to the United States in search of work is not unemployment but rather the real possibility of obtaining greater income, given the development of the American capitalist system. Furthermore, for certain groups, this migration is part of culture; it is a way of life.

At present the phenomenon of Mexican migration is considered to be a serious problem for the United States. That country has attempted to measure the volume of the migratory flow by means of a series of studies whose different methods have not provided specific figures.

The United States has practiced a kind of restrictionism through legislative measures, court ordinances, and selective application of the immigration laws, among others, as well as by stimulating awareness on the part of employers so that they will reject this kind of manpower. I would also point to amnesty proposals and temporary work programs.

In brief, the measures proposed by the United States to date can be grouped into three trends: one of conditional opening of the United States border to the immigration of Mexican workers; another tending toward a relative termination of the immigration; and finally, one that tends toward a control of the flow of migratory workers, based on a recognition of a real demand for foreign manpower from the United States and a surplus of unskilled labor from Mexico, which can only be rectified on a long-term basis.

Furthermore, Mexico's Global Development Plan, which brings together a series of plans and programs, constitutes the Mexican government's response to the country's economic and social problems. The plan institutes a series of basic projects, the most important of which are the National Employment Program, the development of the Mexican Food System, the reduction of demographic growth rates, and the National Productivity Program. Although this plan was not conceived as a response to what the United States calls the migratory "problem," its implementation will definitely contribute to a better handling of the phenomenon.

Both legal and clandestine immigration are considered to be responses to the unequal development of the economies, the goods, and the resources of the two countries.

Thus, there are indications that the migratory flow will continue because the basic structure that caused the movement will not change rapidly; it must be seen as a natural long-range aspect of the growing structural interdependence between the two countries and their respective economies.

The development of a conceptual consensus and organization between the two countries as a prerequisite for substantive discussion is the first step toward cooperation. The next step, according to the thesis of the Mexican government, is the evaluation of specific bilateral issues, not according to the individual interests of each nation, but according to the impact that they have on Mexican-American relations as a whole.

In conclusion, the creation of a new framework for Mexican-American interdependence requires greater understanding of the structural ties between the two countries, with emphasis on economic ties and association of interests. This path presents substantial challenges; but grand schemes will not be fruitful if they are not developed step by step in mutually beneficial negotiations on specific issues.

Dr. Belsasso would like to acknowledge the contributions to the writing of this chapter by Yolanda Isoard and would like to thank Geronimo Martines, Carlos Zazueta, and Cesar Zazueta of the National Center of Labor Information and Statistics (CENIET) and Margarita Dieguez, Olga Salimas de Valle, and Delfina Dubon de Archer of the Ministry of Labor for their valuable orientation and the basic materials for the development of this chapter.

David D. Gregory

7

A U.S.-Mexican
Temporary Workers Program

The Search for Co-Determination

> *The population dynamics of the developed coun-*
> *tries pose the central problem of our turbulent*
> *times. They are, in Shakespeare's term, the "sea-*
> *change." They will have to be managed, and*
> *managed by managers in institutions rather than*
> *left to governments or politicians. As a "social*
> *problem" encompassing the entire economy, the*
> *change may seem unmanageable; but on the local*
> *level, the level of the individual company, the*
> *individual university, the individual industry,*
> *the individual city or region, the problem is*
> *comparatively small, relatively easily managed,*
> *and reasonably inexpensive to solve.*
> —Peter Drucker, Managing in Turbulent Times

DAVID D. GREGORY *is a professor in the Department of Anthropology at Dart-*
mouth College and executive secretary of the Inter-American Council on
Manpower and Development. Dr. Gregory has received several Ford Founda-
tion grants to study immigration in Europe and is author of Andalusian
Odyssey. *He has also written on Mexican immigration for the Senate Judi-*
ciary Committee and the President's Select Commission on Immigration and
Refugee Policy.

Cultural Values and Migration Policy

Some problems seem devoid of a solution because they mirror our traditional sense of values and order. Therefore, we never seem to be able to find the proper answers because we tend to look only in areas of what is already known. The solutions, however, might best be discovered outside the traditional patterns of accepted experience. Such appears to be the case with the dangerous opportunities raised by Mexican migration to the U.S. It is a problem that asks us to question some of our most basic assumptions as a "nation of immigrants." It raises new policy questions that impel us to go beyond our narrow definitions of national sovereignty and seek a new balance between economic opportunities and social pressures. In particular it requires that we make a "cultural shift" in our perceptions that will enable us to view the problem in a larger international context. In terms of public perceptions of Mexican immigration to the U.S. and the economic realities of various regions of the U.S., it is apparent that the problem is not stationary. It continues to grow while the feasibility of our traditional solutions recedes.

THE ANCHOR EFFECT OF HISTORY

Because our long-term history is shrouded in political values and popular sentiments that restrict our view of emigration to problems of permanence and assimilation, it seems unwise to base future U.S. migration policies upon a study of our past. The Select Commission on Immigration and Refugee Policy, entrusted by Congress to recommend changes in U.S. immigration laws, spent much of its existence primarily developing the historical context of the problem. Commentators on all sides of the issue, however, have pointed out that the history of U.S. immigration policy "reflects a national schizophrenia about immigration in a country forged by immigrants." Our immigration laws in today's international environment are antiquated, impractical, and inhumane. For example, the Harboring Law states that if a person shelters, feeds, or supports illegal aliens in his or her home without taking advantage of the aliens' labor or receiving money from them, that person is committing a crime punishable by a $2,000 fine and a prison sentence of up to five years. If, on the other hand, the illegal alien is sheltered and hired, no punishable offense has been committed.

Of course the history of Mexican workers in the U.S. agricultural labor force in the southwestern U.S. is extensive and well-documented. The workers' movement out of agriculture into hotels and restaurants, the garment industry, assembly operations, and health care throughout the U.S. has not been clearly comprehended. In fact, the historical perspective of Mexican participation in earlier programs such as the *bracero* programs acts as an impediment to our current search for a policy to effectively deal with contemporary migration movements.

While accepting the fact that the *bracero* program was to be only a "temporary" movement of agricultural workers, it is difficult for Americans to accept the idea of temporary immigrants throughout the U.S. work force. For U.S. immigration policy temporary immigration is a contradiction in terms in that policy is shaped to handle the legal immigrant as a permanent member of the society. Temporary immigration runs counter to the nation's traditional intellectual and moral framework based upon the popular misconception that immigrants in our past have invariably sought to become permanent U.S. citizens.

In *Birds of Passage*, Michael Piore has graphically illustrated how such popular misconceptions have led Americans to selectively edit their own history. In summarizing the conclusions of the forty-two volume study published by the Immigration Commission of 1911, Piore demonstrates a surprisingly high rate of return migration for the period between 1908–10: 57 percent for Croatians and Slovenians; 63 percent for northern Italians; 56 percent for southern Italians; 65 percent for Magyars; 31 percent for Poles; 41 percent for Russians; 59 percent for Slovaks; 51 percent for Spaniards. Piore quotes the study as saying:

> The New Immigration is very largely one of individuals, a considerable portion of whom apparently have no intention of permanently changing their residence, their only purpose in coming to America being to temporarily take advantage of the greater wages paid for industrial labor in this country. This, of course, is not true of all the new immigrants, but the practice is sufficiently common to warrant referring to it as a characteristic of them as a class. From all the data that are available, it appears that

nearly 40 percent of the new immigration movement returns to Europe and that about two-thirds of those who go remain there. . . .

Today, the U.S. must not only grapple with a growing influx of undocumented illegal aliens but, as in the case of Mexico, large numbers of immigrants seeking temporary residency. Immigration law permits only a trickle of some 20,000 a year to legally emigrate from Mexico to the U.S. The law treats every country equally: Costa Rica as if it were as populous and important to U.S. self-interests as Mexico. The deportations of illegal Mexican migrants, however, are reaching 800,000 annually. Figures on deportations include individuals who have been apprehended more than once in a given year. The fact remains that we really do not know how many illegal Mexicans are currently in the U.S. at any given time. During the Nixon administration the number was estimated at between 6 to 12 million. The Carter Presidency cautiously reduced the estimate to between 4 to 6 million. The most recent study by the Mexican government, discussed by Dr. Belsasso in chapter 6, estimates that there are between 480,000 to 1.22 million undocumented Mexican workers in the U.S.—depending upon the season. This national survey confirms the findings of smaller community studies, like the work of Wayne Cornelius, Josh Reichert, and Douglas Massey, showing the cyclical nature of the movement. It also demonstrates that most of the undocumented migrants in the U.S. intend to return to Mexico and in fact actually do so.

The Mexican figures will be heatedly contested by the various special interest groups in the U.S. There have been no studies in the U.S., however, comparable to that undertaken by Mexico. In the U.S. there has been an epidemic of piecemeal academic, nonaction-oriented studies of the Mexican immigration problem that has led to a rash of inconclusive meetings and seminars. Every aspect of the problem has been pinpointed. Sensitive issues in U.S. domestic affairs, such as the participation of illegal workers in the U.S. social security system, in our educational facilities, in our tax system, have all been examined with no agreement being reached. While the Mexican government has pursued an integrated study of all the aspects of its side of the "migratory chain," our own Select Commission has developed its historical context paying particular attention to the problem of refugees.

Where undocumented, temporary immigrants are concerned, the focus seems to be upon finding ways to increase their difficulties to procure employment in the U.S. It is not always clear to what degree some of their advisors are trying to protect American jobs or American prejudices.

American prejudices often catch the temporary immigrant in a classical "double-bind." It is not uncommon to hear an American say, "We don't want these people here. Why do they come? Why don't they go home?" When informed that the majority will return to where their dollars have greater purchasing power, the same individual will respond, "What's wrong with these ungrateful people? Why do they turn their backs on one of the most democratic, most prosperous countries in the world after having gained so much from it?"

JUST WHOSE PROBLEM IS THIS?

The problem, of course, is not just one of numbers, but of terminology and the powerful emotions the discussion of numbers generates. Migration problems always tend to upset the traditional moral order of any society. This is especially true in the case of return migration for a society like the United States. Americans might begin to question what makes them so angry or afraid in connection with the problem of undocumented, temporary emigration from Mexico? How much longer can we ignore the fact that there are millions of people in the U.S. who are not considered immigrants by either their standards or by our own? Even Mexico does not consider itself an emigrant country no matter how many millions of its citizens cross the 1,945 miles of border into the U.S. Therefore, it might be wise to place less emphasis upon the outmoded term of "immigrant" and its insistence upon permanence, and we might begin to accept such words as "guest worker," "foreign employee," "temporary migrant worker."

There is another way of avoiding the problem besides allowing history to define the present. That is to emphasize the developmental gap between the U.S. and Mexico and place the burden of bridging the gap on Mexico. There are a growing number of studies, *done by Americans*, that prefer to concentrate on the push factors of migration. They assume that we really should not exert too much effort on the U.S. side in trying to deal with the problem because the responsibility for it is in the hands of Mexico. Wayne Cornelius, however, shows in chapter 5 of this volume that Mexico's persistent inability to solve its structural economic difficulties despite growing oil revenues will continue throughout the rest of this century.

No matter how hard we concentrate on Mexico's development gaps, there is no escaping the fact that at least half of the problem is our own. The incentive for Mexican workers to emigrate to the U.S. is predominantly economic. Traditionally, deteriorating economic conditions and increasing demographic pressures in Mexico have positively selected those Mexicans who seek most to help themselves. According to the Mexican CENIET survey, these migrants have a median education higher than the Mexican average and at least three out of four had jobs before being attracted to the U.S. This demonstrates that economic conditions and the supply of labor in Mexico are not sufficient to explain the movement. Rather, one must look at the demand for Mexican labor in the U.S. Changing work habits and participation rates of American citizens in the U.S. labor force and shifting demographic trends will also eventually intensify the problem on the U.S. side by leading to a scarcity of labor which the short-term developments in science and technology will not alleviate.

THE NEW "SEA-CHANGES"

Our short-term history, from the beginning of the Marshall Plan to the mid-1970s, has been an unusual period of economic continuity, rapid growth, and relatively stable economic predictability. According to Peter Drucker and other members of the business community, this period has come to an end. The changes in population structures and dynamics are pushing us into an era of economic, social, and international "turbulence." It is paradoxical that the ensuing decades of unpredictability can be based upon clearly predictable demographic variables: all the major economic actors who will be in the labor forces of the developed and developing countries between now and the year 2000 are now on stage.

Economists and demographers like Peter Drucker, Clark Reynolds, Harold Sheppard, and Sara Rix have shown that by 1990 the dependent population of sixty-five and over in the U.S. will constitute one-eighth of our total population. Those members of our society fifty-five and older will comprise a near-majority of our adult population. Technological advances and higher levels of education in the U.S., combined with the projected short-term demographic trends, will further create a shortage of young workers seeking employment in traditional manufacturing and service jobs. In spite of current rising levels of unemployment, Drucker sees the shortage to be "imminent" because "they expect a career rather than a job. They expect to work as skilled people, and to hold managerial or professional, or at least technical jobs. They are not prepared or qualified, whether technically or mentally, for the traditional jobs of yesterday—for jobs on the farm, in the factory, in the mine, or for any kind of manual work, skilled or unskilled."

Biases in the Search for a New U.S. Immigration Policy

Demographer Kingsley Davis has aptly stated that "whether migration is controlled by those who send, by those who go, or by those who receive, it mirrors the world as it is at the time." Current demographic, economic, and educational trends indicate that the U.S. should begin formulating migration strategies that are openly and honestly based upon our own "enlightened self-interest" as a nation, rather than upon the minority interest of any one particular group. While not abandoning our national commitment to those refugees seeking to escape political tyranny, it is unwise to continue a laissez-faire policy when dealing with the illegal aliens from Mexico who seek temporary employment opportunities. We should address their problems directly rather than hoping that they will be solved by time or through circumstance. We should not let the political problems of thousands of Cubans and Haitians take precedence over the millions of Mexicans who have sought work in the U.S. It seems prudent to honestly consider the interrelationships between migration and economic development with those "developing" countries like Mexico where our economic interests are currently and potentially the most important.

THE STATUS QUO

It is unhealthy to think that we can permit the current situation to continue as is. The assumption that there is a "status quo" that can be maintained is often based on the argument: better the devil you know than the devil you don't know. As Ambassador McBride points out in chapter 1, there is no "status quo." Permissive indifference or benign neglect, which might have constituted policy in the past, augments the number of illegal border crossings with its attendant violence. Furthermore, for the U.S. to condone the current situation is to sanction the large-scale violations of its own laws. Likewise, the "status quo" is a major irritant in our relations with Mexico. It leads to widespread situations involving arrests, violations of human rights, and deportations. This in turn takes a large class of workers who play a significant role in our economy and turns them into a subclass of criminals outside the law. The lack of security, the loss of dignity, and the suffering are not acceptable.

WORK OF THE SELECT COMMISSION AND POLICY RECOMMENDATIONS

While the Select Commission is the first to abjure the "status quo," its recommendations as they now stand still lack the vital component to deal effectively with the difficulties and promises created by undocumented Mexican immigration to the U.S. The Select Commission's definition of the problem continues to be extremely narrow by being fixed on the goal of protecting American jobs and defending minority rights in the work force. In formulating a temporary worker program it appears that the Select Commission proposals concerning U.S.– Mexican migration will rely heavily upon the work of Sidney Weintraub, an economist at the Lyndon B. Johnson School of Public Affairs. Along with stricter border enforcement, his policy proposals are:

> A more vigorous effort to curtail illegal migration to the United States, to be enforced mainly by an employer sanctions program, accompanied by a transition period during which a legal guest worker program of *limited and decreasing size,* eventually decreasing to zero, is instituted in order to moderate the impact of our action on sending nations, primarily Mexico. This would require some form of universal worker identification in order to make the program effective. In the name of equity, the degressive guest worker program should be accompanied by an amnesty program for those aliens already here illegally, and an increase in the number of immigrant visas for nearby countries.

Weintraub believes that the high unemployment experienced by minorities in America can be directly attributed to the presence of illegal workers. Some of us believe that it is more directly the result of a failure in our educational system. Nevertheless, by narrowing their focus on job displacement they have singled out the most controversial issue. Do Mexicans deprive U.S. citizens of jobs? "Yes," say spokesmen for the AFL-CIO, the Labor Department, and many others. "No," say the ranchers, agriculturists, small manufacturers, and many employers in services and health care. The former contend that the presence of Mexican workers in the U.S. is institutionalizing dual labor markets. The latter contend that this might be true but Mexican workers perform jobs Americans will not undertake. A spokesman for the California garment industry has categorically stated that if undocumented Mexican workers were expelled as a body, the industry would close down overnight. It is estimated that a third to a half of the construction workers in Houston are undocumented Mexican workers filling jobs that would go vacant otherwise. Sheldon Maram's interviews with 1,200 unemployed blacks and Hispanics legally in the Los Angeles area showed that few would accept the types of minimum-wage jobs done by undocumented Mexicans.

In fairness to the Weintraub position, it is based on the assumption that every job has its price. His paper, presented to the Select Commission in July 1980, states that "it is hard to believe that there is no price sufficient to attract national workers to what are now undesirable jobs." This position runs contrary to a growing body of evidence in America and grossly oversimplifies what people are trying to maximize through their education and work. I doubt strongly that the associate professor at the University of Pittsburgh would readily exchange his lower paying job for that of a tenured worker at U.S. Steel. A more extreme variant of this position was put forward by Marion Houston of the Department of Labor at a Select Commission hearing on "Seasonal Workers." She went as far as to state that illegal immigration in the U.S. could be "simply" dealt with by getting rid of all the bad jobs in America!

No bad jobs, no illegal immigrants? The mystery of cause and effect continues. Weintraub seems to acknowledge the mystery by admitting that his argument might be refuted by what he calls the "lump of labor fallacy," namely that immigrant labor creates more jobs than it encumbers by reducing bottlenecks and doing the work nationals spurn. He would only accept this argument if a country were facing an *absolute labor shortage*. He cannot accept this in a country like the U.S. with its current rate of unemployment. He then contradicts himself by agreeing that such an absolute shortage is imminent in the next decade and likely to approximate the situation in Europe. There is no real problem, however, because productivity can simply be increased by pumping in more capital. He seems to ignore the fact that capital formation in developed countries is in a decline.

In western Europe, where the problems of an absolute labor shortage have been more prevalent, the debate is more clearly focused upon the relationship between immigration and continued economic growth between the business community and the public sector. Even before the first phase of the energy crisis in 1973, public opinion in the receiving countries had become increasingly hostile toward immigrant workers. Official government policies leaned toward the introduction of new restrictions to meet public protests. However, small and medium-sized employers, as well as large industrialists, continued to push for more immigration. They contended that the slow growth of the labor force would force the governments to decide whether they wanted immigration and continued economic growth or restrictions, repatriations, and economic stagnation. Their arguments were supported by the work of economists like C. P. Kindleberger. Other economists argued that continued immigration was actually inflationary in that it put new pressures on the economy and caused it to overheat. Some of the economists opposed to immigration argued—like Weintraub has argued for the U.S.—that increased automation could substitute for immigrant labor. However, men like Marc Oulin, Renault's secretary general, found that increased automation only created the type of subdivided and repetitive jobs native workers sought to avoid. Jonathan Power, who interviewed Oulin and others, summarized the problem in *Western Europe's Migrant Workers*: ". . . paradoxically, although there is a strong economic case that without immigration jobs would not be done, capital would not work efficiently (night-shift work in particular), upward wage pressures would increase and with it inflation, the populace are looking the other way. Prisoners of their prejudice, even more than their self-interest . . . they demand of their politicians that immigration must stop."

In the U.S. more restrictive policies, like increased border enforcement through the strengthening of patrols and the creation of barriers, ignore that fact that more might be less. These policies lead us into thinking that there is a quantitative answer for what has become a qualitative question. Tougher measures along the border would not only cut off a source of labor which large numbers of U.S. employers

believe necessary to our economy, but they would also have a severe
and negative impact on U.S.–Mexican relations. The emphasis on "amnesty" depending upon the length of stay increases the likelihood of
turning voluntary, temporary migrants into permanent residents. Employer sanctions will have a negative effect upon the economic growth
of many regions and secondary industries in the U.S. They will be
unenforceable in many states, as Senator Harrison Schmidt declared
they would be in New Mexico, and aggravate the single most important problem of the Mexican workers' status: its illegality or criminal-
ity. A universal worker identification card would hurt many of the
minorities the proposals seek to protect. Hispanic Americans in particular believe that it would discriminate against them in the job
market and lay them open to greater police harassment. The strangest
part of the system of proposals is the introduction of some form of
guest worker program for a limited duration of five years. The number of contracts would be reduced each year along with the H-2 visa
program. The demographic and economic realities, however, continue
to argue for a new adaptation and a more just system for the importation of temporary workers rather than an adaptation to the elimination of the jobs they fill. Nevertheless, if the Weintraub position is an
argument for the elimination of the "types" of jobs temporary migrants fill, it is not clear how this will increase employment opportunities for American citizens.

The Need for a New Approach and the Necessary
Background for a Temporary Worker Program

Because of the numbers involved and the unique relationship
between Mexico and the United States, the two countries should undertake a collaborative and thorough study of the agreements which
have been concluded between the labor-exporting nations of southern
Europe and North Africa and the labor-importing nations of the
Common Market and northern Europe. The purpose would be to
ascertain what useful precedents or dangerous pitfalls exist in the
European experience for the U.S. and Mexico. According to Roger
Böhning, of the International Labor Office, and others, there are
enough similarities between the two sides of the Atlantic to permit
cross-national policy learning; this holds true regardless of the fact
that the semisocialistic and parliamentary systems of western Europe

facilitate greater co-determination between business, labor, and government. Most of the receiving countries involved are representative democracies with pluralistic structures, are oriented around a free market economy, and have participated in a system of international economic migration where the volume and direction of migration has been determined more by the demand for workers than by the supply.

At this point, however, such a design must be provisional for the following reasons.

BILATERAL COOPERATION

First, any such design must be provisional because there has not been the proper bilateral consultation with Mexico. Mexico seems willing to be part of a bilateral process. For example, at the First International Meeting of U.S.–Mexican Border Governors in June 1980, there were indications that Mexico might consider joining in such bilateral discussions on migration if the U.S. took the initiative. While no formal or official proposal was made, there were positive indications that Mexico might support some form of temporary worker program in the U.S. as an improvement over current conditions.

Together, we must seek a bilateral agreement, presumably in the form of a treaty, that would be subject to ratification in both countries. Such a treaty would establish the mechanisms for administering a program that would bring Mexican workers to the U.S. for fixed periods of time, at a contracted wage, and in areas of the country where they are most needed. This would not be a new *bracero* program. It would cover large areas of the U.S. as well as employment in manufacturing and service industries.

STUDY EUROPEAN AGREEMENTS

Second, we still lack studies that adequately evaluate the European experiments and their application to the U.S. Most of the studies suffer from the fact that their major focus is upon the years following the crisis of 1973. They ignore or treat lightly the preceding fourteen years of rapid European development and do not fairly consider what the economic course of Germany, France, or Switzerland's growth would have been without this movement of "temporary" workers. Nor do they adequately consider what would have been the continuing eco-

nomic and social stagnation of the temporary workers themselves and
the political unrest in the Mediterranean basin if the workers had
been blocked access to the EEC labor markets. Furthermore, because
of our American heritage which associates assimilation with migration, there has been a tendency for American scholars to focus upon
the problems of the minority of workers and their families who have
remained in the host countries, rather than upon the majority who
have returned home during the past twenty years.

The discrepancy between the views of some of the American re-
searchers and Europeans who are experts in this area was quite apparent in a June 1980 conference on "Temporary Labor Migration
in Europe" sponsored by The World Peace Foundation. Most of the
European studies present a much different picture of such issues as the
number of workers returning home, political rights of aliens, and
second generation immigrants' adaptation to the host countries. For
example, the Americans invariably fall back on the argument that a
guest worker program tends to turn temporary workers into permanent residents. To the contrary, Roger Böhning shows that in Western
Germany between 1961 and 1976, nine out of ten Italians, eight out of
ten Spaniards, seven out of ten Greeks, five out of ten Yugoslavs, and
three out of ten Turks returned home. The Italians with the greatest
return movement were the first to participate in the flow northward.
As members of the Common Market, they were also guaranteed free
movement within the Common Market countries. The Turks were
the last group to participate. They were the farthest from Germany
both geographically and culturally and entered the migratory stream
during the period of declining economic opportunities both at home
and abroad.

In terms of most of the issues related to international economic
migration, the Europeans were amazed by the U.S. system: our virtually open borders, our emphasis upon permanent rather than legal
status, and our concern with amnesty rather than future entrance.

MIGRANT ATTITUDES

Third, there has been little or no attempt to ascertain what the
undocumented Mexican workers' attitudes might be to any form of
temporary worker program. As a temporary workers policy is being
formulated, certain aspects of it should be regionally tested for its

potential acceptance or compliance by the migrants themselves. The Organization of Economic Cooperation and Development (OECD) has been involved in numerous regional and national studies of the various phases of the migration chain in Europe: improving cooperation between employment services in sending and receiving countries; programs for selective return migration; sources of financing for return migration, employment creation, and regional development. One of their major conclusions was:

> All measures undertaken within the framework of the organization of the migratory chain which do not set out from the needs and desires of the individual migrant workers themselves are doomed to failure. The rationale of all the strategies now considered is ultimately to increase the opportunity for choice of the migrants concerned. Thus, a system which does not gain the confidence of the migrant workers, does not provide for the active participation of the representatives of the workers at all levels (planning, implementation, and evaluation) could certainly never prove to be efficient.

EMPLOYER NEEDS

Finally, there have been few direct attempts to consult with the American business community as to their future labor needs and the role that a temporary worker migration program might play in their developmental strategies. If such a program is going to work, it is going to have to have the backing of business. It is business that ultimately does the hiring, will bear much of the cost, and will provide the machinery that will make such a program feasible. I do not think the government or the academic community realizes how seriously the business communities in both Mexico and the U.S. have begun to consider the implications of continued illegal immigration between the two countries. In chapter 4, Al Wichtrich, director-at-large, American Chamber of Commerce of Mexico, clearly demonstrates the basis for this concern. He shows that Mexico is now our third international trading partner. Total dollar volume of trade between Mexico and the U.S. rose from $2.9 billion in 1970 to $19 billion in 1979. This represents 66.8 percent and 65 percent respectively of total Mexican trade. Regardless of the chilly, if not hostile political climate between Washington and Mexico City, trade between the U.S. and Mexico continues. This is all the more impressive since there are no bilateral general trade agreements, just as there are no bilateral labor agreements.

A Sample of U.S. Business Community Attitudes toward the Problem

Ambassador McBride and I have begun to conduct an attitude survey of U.S. business with interests in Mexico. These opinions, particularly well-articulated by a senior manager of a large computer firm involved in marketing in Latin America, are summarized as follows.

1. The relationship between Mexico and the U.S. in the next couple of decades might be not only one of the most important factors in either harmony or disorder on the North American continent, but also in the relationship of developing and Third World countries toward the U.S.

2. By the year 2000, Mexico will have more than half of the population of the U.S. and several times the population of Canada, will have a considerable gross national product, and will be an important market for U.S. products.

3. Presuming that the present effort of the Mexican government to decrease the birth rate to some two-thirds of the present rate by the year 2000, and assuming that its development plans for labor-extensive industry will succeed, Mexico will still have a very large percentage of unemployed and underemployed in the next two decades.

4. Due to the unemployment and high expectation of a better standard of living than the economy will be able to deliver, Mexico should expect social and political unrest to increase in the next two decades.

5. The U.S., being the "rich, powerful" neighbor with past relations sometimes less than friendly, will certainly be blamed by Mexican political and social extremists for slow social development, unemployment, etc.

6. It is, therefore, certainly in the interest of the U.S. to take all possible actions now to decrease the future possible and probable difficulties in relation to Mexico.

7. Illegal Mexican immigrants and overall immigration of Mexicans to the U.S. are certainly obstacles to better relations and are among the most important and unfortunately emotional subjects of the American-Mexican relationship. A large part of the population in the United States feels that there is no obligation to Mexican people to bring them to the United States either as temporary workers or per-

manent residents. It is understandable that they probably feel that the first obligation is to the "U.S. poor and minorities." Unfortunately, the problems of the poor and minorities are a result of our educational system, which has never adequately met their needs, rather than our migration policies.

8. It seems that the Mexicans have not forgotten that they lost a large portion of their territories to the United States and, therefore, feel that the United States has an obligation to help Mexico to absorb a labor force which cannot find jobs in Mexico.

9. In the future, immigration policies toward Mexico cannot be made on the basis of "rights or obligations," but on benefits to both parties.

General Suggestions for a Temporary Workers Program

There are both economic and social limits to any country's ability to absorb immigrants. Invariably the social limits seem to be reached far before the economic ones. Such is the case in western Europe where the various countries are having to make decisions between continued immigration, economic growth, and increasing social unrest. In any case, every country must have a comprehensive and flexible migration policy that attempts to adjust the supply and demand of labor between neighboring countries. If people are brought into a country, they should be brought into a viable job market. The introduction of some variant of a temporary workers program would provide the flexibility the U.S. now seems to lack.

Any temporary workers program for the U.S. should be of a bilateral nature with Mexico, with whom we have mutual economic and social self-interests. Any bilateral agreements between Mexico and the U.S., however, must also be based upon regional needs within both nations. In focusing upon the national effects of immigration, it is important not to forget that the contemporary movement of migratory labor between Mexico and the United States is ultimately a regional problem. By primarily speaking about migration in terms of nation states, we tend to formulate national policies that have little to do with the realities of the internal distribution of population, jobs, and income. While in the short term, national policies seem to have the advantage of being based upon considerations of equity, in the long term they can aggravate regional differences and undermine economic growth.

This is blatantly evident when considering the growth of the region formed by the California-Texas axis. William Stevens, in a *New York Times* article, finds these states to be reshaping regionalism in the U.S. and providing a base for the second stage of development in business and politics. As the first and third most populous states in the U.S., California and Texas are rapidly overtaking the Northeast, not only in population but in economic supremacy as well. Stevens emphasizes that:

> as manufacturing and the influx of nineteenth-century European immigrants largely defined the modern character of the Northeast, so Texas and California, mainly Southern California, are being jointly defined, in a large part, by energy production, agriculture, military and high technology; by increasingly similar middle-class lifestyles and values, and not less, by the emergence of Mexican-Americans as a social and political force.

It is no wonder that the Southwest is dubious about the major role the East Coast plays in formulating future international migration policy.

This regional nature of the immigration problem was highlighted at the recent border governors' meeting. Governor William Clements of Texas defended a position in favor of a temporary worker program. He strongly countered statements that the governors were incorrectly trying to play roles in matters that really pertained to the federal government. Governor Clements maintained that there were many local issues (migration issues, border industries, in-bond warehouses, etc.) that were really within the scope of state administration.

While being sensitive to regional problems, the final policy must be formulated by the federal government. The various branches of the federal government, however, should act primarily as facilitators rather than arbitrators in assisting the regions and states. A workable policy should be designed in the form of a labor treaty negotiated between the Departments of State in the U.S. and Mexico. The Department of Labor, in cooperation with American business, should take on an administrative role. The Department of Justice should be freed to pursue mainly an enforcement role.

Before implementing such a program, proper screening of current undocumented Mexican workers in the U.S. should be carried out. Those who desire to stay permanently and become U.S. citizens in five years could be provided with a "permanent residence" status. Before these are granted, however, the Mexican government should agree that those who have not passed the screening and received "permanent" status can be returned to Mexico. The concept of granting amnesty should be discarded. Its emphasis upon bestowing a general pardon or immunity for past offenses indirectly continues to identify the migrants as a class of ex-criminals forming a separate social group in the United States. Rather than amnesty, we should consider adapting policies to "regularize the status" of undocumented workers from Mexico, policies similar to what the French followed in adjusting the status of hundreds of thousands of Portuguese who entered France without documentation. Special immigration quotas might also first be established for Mexico for a longer period of time. The visa to immigrate might be based upon the following consideration: Mexicans with close relatives currently in the United States who are either citizens or permanent residents, and those who have a clear desire to become permanent U.S. residents after five years.

Only after screening and the establishment of new quotas does it seem feasible to enter into bilateral consultation with Mexico in the designing of a temporary worker program. There should be a long-range plan agreed to between the governments and the business communities as to the number of workers, the occupations to be filled, and the length of stay. The quotas should be based upon the ability of the U.S. economy to effectively employ temporary Mexican workers.

At present, I see no way of establishing the number of visas upon yearly quotas without basing the visas upon the availability of a work contract. Without some form of contract it will be difficult to control for regional and sectorial needs. Most migrants and employers, however, would probably prefer some variation of Wayne Cornelius's proposal which maximizes the freedom of movement of the temporary workers.

To avoid the problems of local administrative irregularities within Mexico, visas should be issued by the U.S. Consulates. The terms of the visa might be determined by the type of contract and job training required in agriculture, manufacturing, or services. The cost of transportation from the border to the place of employment should be paid by the employer. We still need to investigate what type of restriction —if any—should be placed upon the completion of the first contract. The contract can be broken if the employer fails to abide by his side of the agreement or by reimbursement of the travel fee to the employer from the migrant. At that time, the temporary worker should be free to seek new employment. While in the U.S. the temporary workers should share the same benefits and protection as the native workers. They should be incorporated in group health insurance plans where they work. If the temporary workers quit before the completion of their contract, they should not receive unemployment benefits while searching for a better job. If, however, they are laid off before the completion of the contract, they should receive the same unemployment benefits as U.S. citizens working at the same level. If after a specified period of time, they cannot find new employment, they should be encouraged to return to Mexico where they can continue to collect unemployment compensation for six weeks. If they continue without work in the U.S. and do not want to return to Mexico, unemployment compensation can be terminated in the U.S. For those who have completed their contracts, various aspects of the social security system should be studied to find further means of positive reinforcement to assist the temporary workers in their decision to return home.

Second and third visas should be issued upon proof that the temporary workers have successfully completed the contract. Temporary workers should not be encouraged to bring their families until they receive their third visa and are sufficiently familiar with United States society. Upon completion of the wife's second term in the U.S., permission should be given to bring the children if so desired. The adjustment of status for temporary workers and their families should always be made possible. It should, however, go through a series of stages that would take at least five years.

To date, our sample from the business community in the U.S. has emphasized that the most important part of any temporary workers program should center upon vocational training of the immigrants. The larger business enterprises in particular see that the training of temporary workers in the U.S. could lead to new types of "production sharing" and increased transnational economic integration. With Mexico, the United States should create special programs to help the Mexican workers learn the necessary skills in the United States that would be of use for the development of Mexico: services, agricultural programs, professional and manufacturing specialties, and personnel skills. To initiate these training projects, the cooperation of both governments, the business communities, and training institutions would be essential. The cost of such programs should be funded by the governments and industries in both countries that would benefit the most from such programs.

Conclusion

For the various reasons already stated, the United States is in no position to either rule out or accept a temporary workers program. In western Europe there are many variations of such programs from country to country. The United States and Mexico remain largely unaware of these diversities and tend to lump them into one or two models. It is useless to propose or deny a temporary workers program until a more thorough and unbiased comparison of all these European programs is carried out.

Finally, no solution to the problem of undocumented Mexican workers is possible unless a greater effort is made to educate public opinion to the new demographic and economic realities facing the Western Hemisphere. The basis of this education must derive from a new type of co-determination between government, the business community, and labor. This type of co-determination does not mean a more direct sharing in the actual management of U.S. business. It does emphasize, however, the need for all three groups to take other than an adversary role. New channels of communication must be opened between the three sectors of our society if we are to turn the crisis of Mexican immigration into an opportunity for both countries.

William B. Cobb

8

Tourism as a Positive Factor
in the Mexican Economy
and in Mexican Foreign Relations

*Tourism promotes friendship, projects an image
of social stability, and creates economic growth.*
—Miguel Alemán

Mexico, one of the fastest growing tourist destination countries
in the world, in the first six months of 1979 became the number one
country for air travel from the United States. In fact, figures published
by the World Tourism Organization for 1978 reveal that Mexico's
annual receipts for tourism were approximately $1.1 billion, a growth
of 28 percent over the previous year and virtually double the average
growth world-wide.

The President of Mexico, Jose Lopez Portillo, has placed, since his
inauguration, the highest priority on the continued development of

WILLIAM B. COBB *has been director of the Mexican Government Tourism
Office in Washington, D.C., since 1976. Mr. Cobb joined the U.S. Foreign
Service in 1945. He was stationed around the world in six embassies and,
on three occasions, served with the Department of State in Washington,
D.C. He was also first secretary (transportation and communications officer)
of the U.S. Embassy in Mexico before transferring in 1973 to the Economic
Bureau of the Department of State as assistant chief of the Aviation Nego-
tiations Division.*

tourism to Mexico as one of the major factors of the country's economy. Coordination of the tourist sector is carried out by Secretary of Tourism Rosa Luz Algría, in office since August 1980. The Ministry of Tourism is in charge of planning and coordinating all promotional activities with the thirty-one Mexican State Tourist Delegations. It serves as a parent entity which directs all the development activities of the tourist delegations in relation to the economy as a whole, in the development of infrastructure facilities, etc.

The job of promoting Mexican tourist destinations overseas is the task of the Mexican National Tourism Council, whose president is former Mexican President Miguel Alemán Valdés. With thirty-four offices world-wide, known as Mexican Government Tourism Offices, the council actively promotes Mexico's diverse tourist destinations by means of advertising in print media, television, and radio in its primary markets, specifically the United States and Canada.

Tourism has definitely become one of the most important areas of Mexico's economy. For instance, tourism in 1980 was expected to account for approximately $1.6 billion or 38 percent of the nation's balance of payments and around 6 percent of the country's gross national product (GNP). Mexico's overall GNP growth was expected to be approximately 12 percent, but its tourism growth was targeted to show a 17 percent annual increase over 1979, accounting for 10 to 12 percent of the GNP by 1985.

At this writing, Mexico has the largest tourist industry in Latin America. World-wide it is fourth in tourist income ($1.43 billion) and sixth in the number of visitors (4.3 million arrivals). Mexico is committed to long-term tourism development for domestic and foreign reasons. Initially, Mexican tourism was focused on its potential as a foreign exchange earner, and its potential to create jobs. With the rising standard of living and increased leisure time, it is expected that national tourism will be as important to the nation as foreign tourism, making this activity less dependent on foreign markets.

Tourism in Mexico benefits all sectors. It touches labor, agriculture, transportation, energy, banking, water resources, electricity, and communications. The development of tourism as a major factor in Mexico's economic development is guided by the following objectives:

1. to satisfy the right to leisure and recreation of all national residents,
2. to consolidate the strategic role of tourism in the economy (short-term goal, 1976 to 1982),

3. to reach overall efficiency in the function of tourism as an industry (medium-term goal, 1982 to 1985), and
4. to achieve financial and commercial autonomy for the sector as a whole (long-term goal, 1985 to 2000).

From 1977 through 1979, about 12 million tourists have visited Mexico. For the same period, there was a total of 180 million border crossings by people visiting the country from frontier cities and towns. This last activity resulted in $10 billion worth of transactions. In 1979, tourism produced a record year. Gross revenues were up 25 percent, totaling $29.7 billion, in comparison to 1978, making this activity second only to oil as the largest generator of foreign exchange.

For 1980, Mexico expected an overall increase in tourism arrivals of approximately 9.5 percent, totaling 4.6 million tourists, *of which 85 percent come from the United States,* 5 percent from Canada, and the remaining 10 percent from Latin America, Europe, and Asia.

COMPARATIVE DATA, 1976–79

Arrivals	—1976: 3.1 million
	—1979: 4.2 million
	Represents an increase of 35 percent
Revenues	—1976: $835.6 million
	—1979: $ 1.4 billion
	Represents an increase of 65.3 percent
Domestic Tourist Expenditures	—1976: $1.2 billion
	—1979: $1.5 billion
	Represents an increase of 30.6 percent

Mexico has organized tourism development in a very unique manner, and the following sections attempt to clarify and describe the diverse operational areas the tourism sector defines as a way of rationalizing policy-making considerations.

Federal Tourism Law

Submitted to the Chamber of Deputies on December 29, 1979, and approved on February 4, 1980, the Federal Tourism Law enables tourism planning and development to proceed in a more constructive and organized manner than was the case before its existence. The law itself consists of eight chapters and a total of 104 subheadings related specifically to the many factors involved with the tourism industry in general. It provides the following definition of tourism:

> Tourism is a group of activities originated by those who voluntarily travel or plan to travel, for recreational, health, rest, culture, or any other related activity.

The purpose of the law is embodied in the following:

1. planning and programing of tourism activities; promotion of both the external and internal tourist demand as well as the development of appropriate tourist facilities and infrastructure;
2. the creation, conservation, protection, and full use of all available tourist resources of the nation;
3. regulation and control of the principal tourist activities and related services;
4. provision for legal process to all justified complaints related to the consumer of tourist services;
5. establishment, at an equal standing, of the service aspect of tourist activities to the effect that there should be no discrimination on the basis of race, sex, political or religious orientation, nationality, or social condition of those soliciting tourist services.

The tourism secretary is responsible for:

1. elaborating and coordinating of the National Tourism Plan with the appropriate entities and the outline of specific programs for the development, organization, and vigilance of all tourism development activities;
2. organizing and updating the National Tourist Inventory which details all goods, services, and attractions available for the development of tourist activities;
3. providing and compiling tourism statistics;
4. making sure that all tourist facilities satisfy the quality requirements, pertinent to each specific case, as established in Mexican laws and regulations;
5. providing its point of view in the acceptance of foreign investment in tourism-related projects;
6. informing the secretary of finance and public credit which tourism investments should benefit from fiscal incentives in accordance with the law;
7. authorizing prices and fees of principal tourist services, with the exception of passenger transportation costs;

8. intervening as the representative of the Mexican government in the development and acceptance of cooperative agreements with interested foreign governmental and/or private sector enterprises with proven interest in tourism-related activities;

9. formulating and implementing all necessary measures for the development of social tourism; and

10. promoting the creation of agrarian centers which will foster the production of consumer goods for the areas of tourist development as well as the establishment of distribution systems for the same.

The Federal Tourism Law is implemented through a system of governmental action and coordination denominated SIPLANTUR. SIPLANTUR assures the rationalization of tourism development at all levels, mandatory at federal and state levels and indicative for the private sector. It also indicates the most convenient way of investing the country's social, economic, and technical resources in the field of tourism.

Under SIPLANTUR the country has been divided into fourteen regions, a logical segmentation which eventually attempts to channel all development credits, financial incentives, and tax deductions to areas which demand economic development for a more balanced economic growth. The final document containing the regulations of SIPLANTUR was finalized in August 1979.

FONATUR (Fondo Nacional de Fomento al Turismo)

FONATUR, Mexico's governmental development agency for tourism, appears as a separate chapter of the Federal Tourism Law. Mario Moy Palencia is the director general of the fund, whose headquarters are located in Mexico City.

FONATUR, a financial trust, operates in accordance with the Federal Tourism Law, the contract signed with the secretary of finance and public credit, and the operational regulations established by the technical committee of fund disbursement of the secretary of tourism. In addition, FONATUR advises and develops financial and promotional programs, fostering in this manner the development of national tourist activities in accordance with the SIPLANTUR.

In order to fulfill its objectives, FONATUR complies with the following responsibilities:

1. fosters the formation and development of Mexican enterprises in the tourism field;
2. effectuates the development of new areas of tourist interest, tourist resorts, as well as fostering the development of those areas in existence at the present time;
3. promotes, fosters, and orients public and private investment to areas of tourism development, particularly new projects;
4. acquires, urbanizes, develops, sells, rents, and administers real estate properties used in tourism projects;
5. provides guarantees in specific cases related to loans provided by credit institutions to individuals dedicated to the tourist industry or related activities;
6. warrants, when required, the amortization and payment of interest of obligations or bonds floated by financial institutions with the purpose of fostering tourist development with the resources obtained;
7. acquires financial obligations and bonds of financial institutions for the development of tourist services;
8. discounts titles of financial credit institutions originating credit provided to individuals dedicated to the tourist industry or similar activities;
9. provides credit to individuals, trade societies, civic associations, cooperatives, and other social and economic entities dedicated to tourist activities;
10. provides credit directly for the financing of tour packages and plans related to social tourism efforts which receive the approval of the secretary of tourism;
11. administers, in individual accounts, the social security and savings funds of tour guides and others related to FONATUR as stipulated in the operational contract.

The resources of FONATUR are composed of:

1. the financial contributions determined by the federal government;
2. the financial resources obtained from the Federal District Department;
3. state and municipal entities;
4. other enterprises which wish to contribute, such as public and private corporations;
5. the credits obtained through prior approval of the secretary of finance and public credit, from national and foreign funds; and
6. funds obtained as a result of its own operational activities.

FONATUR has a technical committee of fund disbursements com-

posed of a president, in this case the secretary of tourism, and representatives of the secretary of finance and public credit, the secretary
of patrimony and industrial development, the Banco de México
(Mexico's central banking authority), and the Nacional Financiera
S.A. The director general of FONATUR is appointed by the President of the United Mexican States.

FONATUR provides credit support, particularly to luxury hotels,
for developing infrastructure facilities, such as roads; basic services,
such as electricity, potable water, telephone communications; and
lodging which will be later sold or rented. It discounts up to 90 percent of credits with maximum repayment periods of up to fifteen
years and three-year grace periods. Its interest rates are between 14
and 22.5 percent depending on the total amounts of the loan.

Between 1977 and 1979, FONATUR had financed the construction
of 2,183 rooms in 1977; 8,347 in 1978 (+282.36 percent); and 9,753 in
1979 (+16.84 percent). Its credit operations for the same period were
$56.9 million in 1977, $134.1 million in 1978 (+135.67 percent), and
$147 million in 1979 (+9.62 percent) (see Table 1).

FONATUR has identified the following areas for the construction
of hotel rooms: Central Valley, 15,110 rooms; the states of Michoacan
and Jalisco, 11,440 rooms; Acapulco, 11,070 rooms; and the Caribbean, 10,000 rooms. To date, Mexico has added 37,860 rooms and
twelve tourism complexes all in a period of three years. According to
the secretary of tourism, it is expected that another 60,000 rooms will
be added to the already extant 231,590 hotel rooms by the end of
1982. The goal for construction for the period 1977 to 1982 is for
97,000 new hotel rooms (see Table 2).

TOURISM INVESTMENT

Despite Mexico's rate of inflation and its impact on hotel prices and
tourism-related services, the nation's tourism industry is flourishing
and has remained competitive because of much higher prices in other
tourist centers. This has been a direct result in many cases of the high
price of energy.

With the high goal of hotel room construction, it is no wonder that
national and international hotel chains are moving into the construction of new resort areas, hotels, and condominiums, all amount-
ing to a sizable amount of capital investment.

TABLE 1. BANKING INSTITUTIONS WHICH BENEFITED FROM CREDITS OBTAINED
FROM FONATUR, 1978

Name of Bank	Number of Credits	Quantity (Mexican pesos in thousands)
Banamex	22	1,366,545.0
Somex	9	362,100.0
Bancomer	25	340,695.9
Multibanco Comermex	19	304,048.0
Banco Mexicano	9	130,300.0
Unibanco	3	72,500.0
Banco del Atlantico	1	60,000.0
Nafinsa	9	58,315.0
Banpais	1	50,000.0
Banpacífico	2	42,000.0
Bancam	3	40,200.0
Banca Sofimex	1	35,000.0
Banco Industrial de Jalisco	3	34,500.0
Banco Internacional	2	28,000.0
Banca Serfín	3	28,000.0
Banco de Puebla	1	20,000.0
Banca Confía	1	15,000.0
Banco de Occidente de México	1	15,000.0
Banco Minero y Mercantil	2	13,360.0
Financiera Sofimex	1	12,000.0
Banco Internacional de Tamaulipas	1	11,000.0
Banco Internacional Peninsular	1	10,500.0
Banco del Ahorro Nacional	1	5,000.0
Banco del Centro	1	4,000.0
Banco Internacional del Centro	1	2,500.0
Financiera Michoacana	2	2,300.0
Banco del Noroeste de México	1	2,100.0
Financiera Peninsular	1	2,000.0
Financiera de Agricultura y Transportes	1	2,000.0
Banco Popular	1	2,000.0
Financiera Potosina	1	1,100.0
Banco General de Tamaulipas	1	1,000.0
Banco Comercial Peninsular	1	800.0
Banco Longoria	1	715.0
Financiera Industrial	1	250.0
Direct Credits:	1	10,230.0
Totals:	135	3,085,058.9

TABLE 2. AUTHORIZED CREDIT DISTRIBUTION BY STATE, ROOMS FINANCED,
AND TOTAL EMPLOYMENT GENERATED, 1979

State	Rooms Financed (Includes Remodeled)	Direct Employment Generated
Federal District	1,533	793
Guerrero	1,058	981
Jalisco	1,656	1,318
Quintana Roo	741	586
Queretaro	380	490
Sinaloa	589	400
Tabasco	212	138
Baja California Norte	386	234
Veracruz	544	232
Chiapas	540	239
Oaxaca	290	184
Baja California Sur	27	24
San Luis Potosí	322	160
Colima	151	65
Guanajuato	389	123
Tamaulipas	225	65
Puebla	40	27
Coahuila	98	35
Hidalgo	60	19
Michoacán	164	5
Chihuahua	52	18
Neuvo León	80	19
Sonora	18	13
Tlaxcala	10	5
Campeche	26	14
Aguascalientes	46	23
Total:	9,526	6,220

Source: FONATUR, 1979.

For example, in March 1980, FONATUR launched a new program
geared to provide larger amounts of credit for hotel projects built by
Mexicans without foreign capital. This strategy is aimed at developing lodgings which will cater to the average Mexican traveler, leaving
the big, high-class projects to joint ventures between large Mexican
industrial groups and foreign capital.

The reasoning behind this new investment program was a direct
result of a study revealing that eight times as many Mexicans as for-

eigners vacation in the country. In addition, FONATUR is providing short-term and medium-term credits to labor unions and other groups to finance vacations for their members in accordance with the development of social tourism.

FONATUR is also pouring massive funds into the development of top-class resorts in Cancun, Ixtapa-Zihuatanejo, San José del Cabo, Loreto in Baja California, and Puerto Escondido in the state of Oaxaca. As of 1981, investment in the area exceeded $280 million.

The areas receiving greatest attention are the Caribbean Coast, the south of Cancun in the state of Quintana Roo, Cozumel, the Baja Peninsula, the Sea of Cortés, the Pacific Coast, and the states of Guerrero and Oaxaca.

Overall, a total of $3.1 billion is planned as investment in hotel construction up to the mid-1980s. The hotel chains involved in this massive development are Western International (Camino Real), Holiday Inns (Posadas de México), Nacional Hotelera (Hoteles El Presidente), Calinda (Banamex/Quality Inns of America), Hilton Hotels (Multibanco Comermex), Aristos, Club Med, Fiesta Americana, and Hyatt Regency.

Tourist development covers the entire country. The following geographic areas describe what is planned during the 1980s.

Caribbean Area—Italy's Manfredi Group, in association with Mexican federal tourist organizations and the secretary of tourism, will begin work on a $201 million project to construct a huge vacation complex at the Caleta de XEL-HA in the state of Quintana Roo. In Cancun, the Cancun Sheraton recently opened with 322 rooms. Five hotels are being built by El Rosario Corporation, Inmobiliaria Hotelera de Yucatán, Promotora Hotelera Misión, Marsa Corporation, and Visión S.A.

Central Pacific Coast Area—in the Bay of Tenacatita, a $173 million tourist center is planned. On the coast of the state of Jalisco, a project is being undertaken involving three thousand hotel and condominium rooms, a yacht harbor, and a communications center. In addition, in the state of Nayarit, new land is being developed for hotels and condominiums. North of Puerto Vallarta in Punta Careyes, the Hotel Plaza Careyes is expanding at a multimillion dollar cost.

Southern Pacific Coast Area—In Ixtapa, state of Guerrero, five hotels will open this year, representing a total investment of more than $74 million. They are the Camino Real, Krystal Ixtapa, Dorado Pacífico, Club Med, and an unnamed resort run by Promotora Hotelera.

North Pacific Area—The Banco Nacional de México (BANAMEX) and Business Men's Assurance Company are investing over $201 million in the construction of a resort complex on the Isla de Piedra, off the coast of the city of Mazatlan in the state of Sinaloa. Across the Sea of Cortés, in the state of Baja California Norte, California Associates has begun work on "El Girasol," part of a tourist complex expected to involve an overall investment of $746 million.

National Development Projects—Still undefined as to location, PRO-TELS, a joint venture involving France's Wagon Lits International and Mexico's Banco del Atlántico, will begin construction of more than three thousand rooms. In the same regard, Quality Inns of America, in association with Banco Nacional de México, is initiating an ambitious program consisting of forty hotels across the nation. Hilton Hotels, in association with Multibanco Comermex, will begin construction of several hotels totaling 1,500 rooms. Meridien Hotels, a subsidiary of Air France, plans construction of seven hotels totaling $750 million worth of investment.

EMPLOYMENT RESULTING FROM TOURISM

As is well known, the investment required for the creation of jobs in tourism is low in relation to industry and other specialized sectors. This is one of the reasons the Mexican government has placed such a high value on tourism development as a means of creating jobs. At present, the tourist industry of Mexico employs approximately 1.4 million people for which 850,000 jobs were created on a direct basis.

It is expected that between 1979 and 1982, a total of 600,000 jobs will be created in the tourism industry. Between 1982 and 1985, a total of 700,000 jobs will result from the tourism industry alone. In 1985, the total number of jobs resulting from tourism will employ about 2.2 million workers.

In addition to jobs, training is involved for persons working in the tourism industry. At present, Mexico has over 220 tourism schools with a range of careers from one to four years to cover a range from the basic needs of the hotel industry to the needs of specially trained professionals in planning and development.

Mexico places high priority on this aspect of tourism development due to its high rate of population growth, particularly in the labor force, and therefore foresees the benefits tourism employment can provide. It should be noted that the construction of one hotel room accounts for approximately 1.8 direct jobs and 2 indirect jobs.

Social Tourism

Within the social fiber of Mexican society, a great majority of the population cannot enjoy the available tourist services, the main factor being the inability to pay the high costs of consumpti' ı. This is evident because the general wage level is low.

To remedy this situation partially and to fulfill the objectives of the Federal Tourism Law, social tourism's prime responsibility is to provide to the majority of national residents the ability or the means to participate, in an economic sense, in tourist-related activities in order to achieve a greater sense of identity and national solidarity through the appropriate usage of the nation's touristic patrimony for the benefit of all. It is believed that social tourism will further stimulate economic activity by fostering the formation of cooperatively based enterprises, which will be made up of firms providing services for the users of tourist services, and cooperatives whose members will be the tourists themselves.

The secretary of tourism supports the concept of social tourism through the Dirección General de Turismo Social which is in charge of increasing basic facilities; developing programs; and forming cooperative societies, associations, and committees which will promote this type of social activity. Furthermore, the programs promoted by the secretary of tourism in this area obtain preferential credit treatment, and those investors who participate in the development of social tourism facilities also receive preferential treatment.

Since social tourism is the new wave of touristic development in Mexico, given its immense growth potential and the fact that it offers preferential treatment in transportation costs, lodging, and other tourist services, this has prompted the development of tourist service entities within federal and state governmental agencies. For instance, the ISSSTE (the Mexican Social Security Agency for Government Workers) has its own travel bureau known as TURISSSTE, which operates as a travel wholesaler providing a wide range of economically priced excursions. This is only the beginning of a massive touristic superstructure which will, in future years, meet the high demands for tourist services by the millions of Mexicans now unable to enjoy the existing facilities, at the moment out of their economic reach.

Foreign Relations

In the field of international relations, the tourism promotion carried on outside the country by the Mexican Government Tourism Offices and the acceptance of the theme "Mexico, the Amigo Country" have created, in the opinion of many, a favorable image of Mexico with regard to its numerous tourist destinations. Mexico's touristic image is widely diffused through advertising and the distribution of promotional literature, such as millions of brochures and thousands of posters. The investment cost in the previously mentioned areas is worth mentioning since a total of 1.6 billion people are expected to see or read the product of Mexico's advertising campaign in the U.S. and Canada. The total dollar figure for advertising in 1980 surpassed the $7 million mark.

Another area of importance in Mexico's foreign relations is the signing of bilateral tourism agreements. To date, Mexico has signed bilateral tourism cooperation agreements with the following countries:

- Brazil (signed July 24, 1974)
- Venezuela (signed March 22, 1975)
- Rumania (signed June 10, 1975)
- Zengal (signed July 13, 1975)
- Spain (signed October 14, 1977)
- Italy (signed January 3, 1978)
- United States (signed May 4, 1978)
- China (signed October 27, 1978)
- Japan (signed November 1, 1978)
- Bulgaria (signed April 6, 1979)
- Colombia (signed June 8, 1979)
- France (signed May 17, 1980)
- Canada (signed June 18, 1980)
- Costa Rica (signed July 25, 1980)

- Brazil (implementing agreement, signed July 29, 1980)
- Cuba (signed August 2, 1980)

No discussion of tourism in Mexico would be complete without reference to the influence which Mexican aviation policies have had on tourism growth. Since 1965, when the government of Mexico agreed to remove capacity restrictions on the operation of scheduled aircraft between Mexico and the United States, the expansion of air services has been of almost explosive dimensions. In 1965, four United States airlines flew to Mexico City, Monterrey, and Mérida. As of November 1980, thirteen United States airlines have the opportunity to link twenty-three U.S. cities with seventeen Mexican cities and resort points, and during the first six months of 1980 Mexico ranked first among foreign destinations visited by air travelers from the United States.

The role played by the two Mexican flag airlines in this market is noteworthy. The privately owned Mexicana Airlines now carries more passengers between the United States and Mexico than any single United States airline. With the largest fleet of 727 aircraft of any airline outside the United States, it now carries almost one-third of the total market between the two countries. Aeromexico, a Mexican government corporation, links Mexico to Europe, South America, and the major United States cities with wide-bodied jet service. Both airlines offer frequent service between scores of Mexican cities at relatively low fares, thus providing an essential ingredient of economic integration for the nation's future growth and progress.

At no time in history has the possibility for strengthening its economic growth looked better for Mexico. While oil will continue to play a major role, development is also taking place in agriculture, marine industries, mineral resources, and commercial and industrial products. Tourism, sometimes referred to as "white petroleum" or "the industry without chimneys," continues to grow apace, thanks to the cooperative efforts of the hotel industry, the airlines, national and international banking interests, and the Mexican government. Although inflation is a factor as real in Mexico as it is anywhere else in the world, Mexico continues to be a good travel value. Travel for vacation purposes has increasingly become a part of man's way of life, and less of a luxury.

The proximity of Mexico to the United States, the hospitality it traditionally offers its visitors, the variety of its scenic beauty, its archeological treasures, and its modern facilities all contribute to the confidence of the tourism industry.

Index

The American Assembly
COLUMBIA UNIVERSITY

About The American Assembly

The American Assembly was established by Dwight D. Eisenhower at Columbia University in 1950. It holds nonpartisan meetings and publishes authoritative books to illuminate issues of United States policy.

An affiliate of Columbia, with offices in the Graduate School of Business, the Assembly is a national educational institution incorporated in the State of New York.

The Assembly seeks to provide information, stimulate discussion, and evoke independent conclusions in matters of vital public interest.

AMERICAN ASSEMBLY SESSIONS

At least two national programs are initiated each year. Authorities are retained to write background papers presenting essential data and defining the main issues in each subject.

A group of men and women representing a broad range of experience, competence, and American leadership meet for several days to discuss the Assembly topic and consider alternatives for national policy.

All Assemblies follow the same procedure. The background papers are sent to participants in advance of the Assembly. The Assembly meets in small groups for four or five lengthy periods. All groups use the same agenda. At the close of these informal sessions, participants adopt in plenary session a final report of findings and recommendations.

Regional, state, and local Assemblies are held following the national session at Arden House. Assemblies have also been held in England, Switzerland, Malaysia, Canada, the Caribbean, South America, Central America, the Philippines, and Japan. Over one hundred thirty institutions have co-sponsored one or more Assemblies.

ARDEN HOUSE

Home of the American Assembly and scene of the national sessions is Arden House which was given to Columbia University in 1950 by W. Averell Harriman. E. Roland Harriman joined his brother in contributing toward adaptation of the property for conference purposes. The buildings and surrounding land, known as the Harriman Campus of Columbia University, are 50 miles north of New York City.

Arden House is a distinguished conference center. It is self-supporting and operates throughout the year for use by organizations with educational objectives.

AMERICAN ASSEMBLY BOOKS

The background papers for each Assembly are published in cloth and paperbound editions for use by individuals, libraries, businesses, public agencies, nongovernmental organizations, educational institutions, discussion and service groups. In this way the deliberations of Assembly sessions are continued and extended.

The subjects of Assembly programs to date are:

1951——United States-Western Europe Relationships
1952——Inflation
1953——Economic Security for Americans
1954——The United States' Stake in the United Nations
——The Federal Government Service
1955——United States Agriculture
——The Forty-Eight States
1956——The Representation of the United States Abroad
——The United States and the Far East
1957——International Stability and Progress
——Atoms for Power
1958——The United States and Africa
——United States Monetary Policy
1959——Wages, Prices, Profits, and Productivity
——The United States and Latin America
1960——The Federal Government and Higher Education
——The Secretary of State
——Goals for Americans
1961——Arms Control: Issues for the Public
——Outer Space: Prospects for Man and Society
1962——Automation and Technological Change
——Cultural Affairs and Foreign Relations
1963——The Population Dilemma
——The United States and the Middle East
1964——The United States and Canada
——The Congress and America's Future
1965——The Courts, the Public, and the Law Explosion
——The United States and Japan

Second Editions, Revised:

DATE DUE

JUN 1 9 '89			